# *Father*

# Please Let Him Live

A true story of losing everything to gain the
only thing.. Jesus

---

Jodi Manfred

FATHER PLEASE LET HIM LIVE:
A True Story of Losing Everything to Gain the Only Thing.. Jesus

Made available by 79 Ministry (www.79ministry.com)

Cover design by: Jodi Manfred

# CONTENTS

*Dedication*                                                                 4

*Intro*      Life's Paintbrush                                               7
             *Dreams Coming True - Tragedy Lurking*

Chapter 1    My Worst Fear                                                  10
             *Invisible Bondage*

Chapter 2    Room 79                                                        22
             *Entering the Valley*

Chapter 3    He Lived                                                       44
             *Conversations from Heaven*

Chapter 4    Purpose in the Pain                                            73
             *Why God?*

Chapter 5    Choose Life                                                   100
             *He makes my paths straight*

Chapter 6    Purple Stones                                                 110
             *His paintbrush is everywhere*

Chapter 7    He Uses the Broken                                            150
             *Lights in the storm*

Chapter 8    Josh Will Walk                                                183
             *The countdown begins*

Chapter 9    It is Finished                                                212
             *He is faithful*

Chapter 10   Be Still                                                      240
             *Healing in the brokenness*

*About the Author*                                                         251

# edication

This book is dedicated to

**Jesus Christ, our Lord and Savior,**

*and to all of those who have shown us his love, acting as the hands and feet of our Lord:*

Josh and I want to express our heartfelt gratitude to JoAnn & Jim Wheat, (my mom and step dad), for parenting our children and taking over our responsibilities at home while we were living in the hospital - also for your continued love and support still today. We want to thank Josh's dad, Jim Manfred for making our home handicap accessible, and for visiting with us every Sunday after church. We want to thank his family: Vivian, Van & Tiffany, Jason & Jess - as well as the families at the Woodlands Church, who prepared meals for us when we returned home from the hospital.

We want to thank Candace & Sean Wheat (Comfortable Home Furnished Apartments) for providing us lodging in the Houston Medical Center. Rani Bivens, you're so kind for setting up a GoFundMe page to help us with medical expenses. Kyle & Jennifer Stephenson: your gift was amazing - my daughter plays that piano nightly, performing worship music for our family. Bryce Stewart, thank you for taking care of my customers while we were away. Blessing and Neha, thank you for being purple stones, (you'll understand later in the book what this means).

# *Special* Dedication to My Granny..

Since I was a little girl, you were always my *one*. And today, more than ever, I see the important role you played in my life. You taught me what unselfish love looks like. You showed me who I want to become. I may not understand why you had to suffer through so much. But, I can only imagine the treasures that were waiting for you up there. I hope one day I can be just half the woman you were.

*You're my hero Granny.* Please pray for me and ask God to give me the strength to finish my race well, so I can see you again, one day soon.

## *Those* who have prayed for us...

I want you to know my eyes are full of tears as I type the words *thank you.* Your faith-filled prayers moved mountains for us, and my heart overflows with deep appreciation for you. You all have shown us how to stand in the gap and intercede for others. You have shown us unselfishness, kindness, encouragement and compassion that continues to shape and mold our hearts today.

## *Those* who are hurting today..

Please know that you aren't alone. We hope and we pray that this book will bless your life, give you encouragement and help you to keep moving forward in Jesus. We invite you to follow us, fellowship with us, cry with us and pray with us on www.79ministry.com.

*We love you all very much.* <3

# *Life's* Paintbrush

## Dreams Coming True - Tragedy Lurking

We paint these pictures of what life will look like in 3 years or 10 years. I was 15 years old when i picked up a colored pencil and scribbled "Josh and Jodi Forever" enclosed in a heart, on the paperback cover that wrapped my history book in first period.

Josh was a senior at Humble High - the guy all the girls swooned over. He was the guy that my mother had warned me about - tall, dark, handsome - dreamy in every aspect of the word, and up to no good.

I still remember the terror on her face when I announced that Josh and I had decided to rent an apartment and move-in together. I was only 17, (going on 30) with no clue about the struggles that stood in my future. But it didn't matter to me. Josh had nothing to offer in terms of stability. He barely graduated high school and college wasn't looking like an option for either of us at the time. But he had the one thing I couldn't live without - *my heart*. I remembered laying in my bedroom at night praying, "God, just give me Josh and I'll never ask for anything again."

Fast forward 20 years later, my paintings that I had kept locked away deep in my thoughts of *happily ever afters* were finally becoming a reality. Josh was still the man of my dreams. He was now 38, wearing a twenty-something year-old body. His strong, muscular frame and baby face turned heads everywhere we went. And even though our current dating life usually consisted of weekends at the youth football fields where Josh coached a group of boys, or attending parent meetings, where I volunteered as President of our school booster club, I felt lucky to be the small-framed blonde wrapped around Josh arm.

We had two beautiful children. My daughter MaeKenna (named after my Granny Mae), was an accomplished honor roll student in her sophomore year of high school. And our son Josh Jr. was a phenomenal athlete - dominating middle school sports as the a-team quarterback at AMS and the lead scorer of our basketball team.

As far as our careers, we were doing amazing. Our journeys in the professional world over the past two decades had been difficult - full of struggle and stress. And early on in our marriage we had endured many Christmas holidays as a family, by pawning items just to scrape up enough money to put a few gifts under the tree for our children. But now, my handsome, strong, athletic, hard-working husband was a successful businessman - just receiving his third promotion in less than three years with Perry Homes. And I wasn't doing so bad myself, ranked in the number three position among realtors in northeast Houston.

It was 2016, and we were starting the year in a new home, with a brand new custom pool, paid in cash. In February, we'd even saved enough money to buy our daughter a luxurious Mercedes C-class for her 16th birthday. I had everything and could afford to lose nothing.

The theme that seemed to sound off on a daily basis inside of my mind was *just keep everything in place, exactly as it is now….* Life was good for the Manfred family…

Little did I know that the impossible was lurking just around the corner, waiting to send our picture-perfect lives into a whirlwind of tragedy and great loss.

Little did I know that my heartfelt prayer I had once laid down before God, as a 15-year old in my bedroom, asking him, "Just give me Josh and I'll never ask for anything again," would soon return to me in the form of a new request. Only this time, I wouldn't just be asking God to give me Josh - I'd be asking God to be merciful, while laying on the cold floor of ICU room #79, whispering, "Father, Please let him live…"

Josh & Jodi
Forever

# $\mathcal{My}$ Worst Fear

## Invisible Bondage

I had heard the phrase often, *"the more you have, the more you have to lose."* For me, losing money or material possessions wasn't frightening. Losing love was. I'd learned at an early age that love can leave - standing in the doorway at only 5 years old, I watched my dad drive away, to never return again. Fast forward 21 years - the amount of love in my life today almost seemed too good to be true. I'd married my high-school sweetheart and we were still going strong after 16 years together - raising two amazing kids. Yet the childhood memory that I carried in the background served as a constant reminder that the very ones I cherish the most, aren't guaranteed inside of my tomorrow. That terrified me to the core.

I don't know how it happened, really. Vacations spent with my family, ruined - because I was too scared to let the kids swim with dolphins or ride the waterslides alone. *What if someone kidnaps them? What if they tragically drown?* I always looked for the *what if*, in every situation.

From the time they were old enough to ride a bike or play in the yard, I began the covering process. I limited their every move, plagued by a consistent video of potential loss and destruction that repeated in my thoughts. I was the over-protective mom that sought to control absolutely everything out of a deep desperation to not lose anything.

Sometimes, I tracked my husband's phone when the weather was bad - often listening to the Harris Country live emergency broadcast. My heart would race each time a motor vehicle accident was reported in close proximity to Josh's path from his office to our home.

My nightly prayer never changed. *God, please protect my family from harm. You say that you'll never give me anything I can't handle -*

*and you know that I could never handle something happening to my kids or my husband.*

"Mom why are you so stressed?" My son, Josh Jr. rolled his eyes as he breezed through the living room into the kitchen. It was a question he'd asked me often - not expecting an answer. For my son, this was his way of sharing his disapproval of my behavior when I would break out into one of my *moments.* Over the last three days, my *moments* had been consistent, as I was terribly worried about my husband, Josh.

It all started on Tuesday night. Josh came home from the gym acting very strange. "Something's wrong with me - something really bad," he confessed as he waved me into our bedroom. Josh explained that he had nearly passed out after entering the gym. He lost his vision, became dizzy and could hardly make his way back to his truck. "Something's very wrong. My head is killing me," Josh muttered, burying his face into his palms.

I took Josh straight to a local emergency room. I couldn't remember Josh ever checking into an ER before. He was too much of a tough guy to do ERs. The fact that he agreed to go with me, immediately ignited my worry. *It must really be serious,* I thought.

Josh was released that night, only to wake up feeling worse the next day. Wednesday afternoon I took him to a different local ER - one of the big hospitals in our area. They too sent him home with a diagnosis of headache and elevated blood pressure. But despite the pain and blood pressure medications, by Thursday morning Josh's condition had reached a new level of extreme.

"I just wish someone would shoot me and take me out of my misery." I opened my eyes from a light sleep to find Josh seated at the foot of our bed, with his head buried in his hands.

"Baby is it that bad?" I jumped down from our bed and dropped to my knees in front of Josh - searching the face he was hiding from me. When I saw tears streaming down his face, I panicked.

11

"You're crying!" I announced. "Oh my gosh, come on let's go! Get up!"

I've known Josh since he was 17 years old and I'd never seen this man cry before - *not once*. There was no doubt in my mind that whatever pain Josh was experiencing, it was a feeling he'd never before known.

"Please hurry! I think I'm having an aneurism!" Josh was hysterical as he repeated the warning that we'd discussed with his mother during our first ER visit. According to Vivian, Josh's aunt died of an aneurism in her early 20's - a tragedy that was initiated by the onset of a terrible headache.

I drove as fast I could back to the emergency room. When we arrived, he immediately opened the passenger side door and started throwing up in the parking lot at the ambulatory entrance. I struggled to help Josh out of the car - positioning my small frame under his left armpit. He could barely walk and his steps were unbalanced, pulling me with him to one side.

"Somebody help us!" I screamed at the large glass doors as a nurse scurried toward us with a wheelchair.

We spent Josh's entire birthday in the emergency room. They ran blood tests and another CT-scan. According to the doctors, the scan of Josh's brain was abnormal - they called it atrophy. Yet, they said the condition wasn't a concern. They kept him in care throughout the day, filling his IV with different drugs in attempt to control his pain and blood pressure.

"Could it be an aneurism? What about his eye? Why is his eyelid drooping like that and why is he complaining that he can't see? Why can't he walk? Why did he almost pass out at the gym? Why is he complaining of the worst headache of his life, despite the pain medicines you're giving him?" I threw questions and concerns at the medical staff, sounding like a broken record, throughout the day.

"It's a migraine mimicking stroke symptoms," was the repeated answer to my long list of continual questions. And even though Josh told the doctors repeatedly, "No, I've had migraines before and they go away with Excedrin. This is different. I feel like my eye is about to explode inside of my head," they dismissed his complaints and reassured us that nothing was seriously wrong with Josh - making side jokes about his impressive physique. "He's the healthiest guy in this room," one of the male nurse's commented. After three long days of battling intense pain, Josh was released to go home, yet again.

On this night, we were supposed to be out together as a family, celebrating Josh's life, in turning 39 years old. But, instead, we were gathered around Josh in our living room. I felt like I was about to be swallowed whole in my worry, as I watched Josh laying on the couch moaning in agony. I called my mother for advice.

Within a matter of minutes her and Jim, (my step-dad), were at our front door. They had recently moved cross country and settled into the house directly behind us. I was glad to have them so close by, to come over and help me with Josh.

My mom immediately went to work on my husband - drenching a rag from the cabinet in cold water and placing it over his head. Josh thanked her, but it was evident that her efforts hadn't provided him any release.

"Did you call the doctor and tell him he's still in pain?" My mother asked, mirroring my worry with her empathic eyes.

"I did. He won't call me back."

Jim tried to keep Josh company as the two sat across the sofa from one another. They both loved talking football and sports - and I appreciated that Jim was at least attempting to take Josh's mind off of his extreme head pain.

"What do you think about their quarterback situation?" Jim asked Josh. I swept the wood floors in the hallway as I followed their conversation - waiting for Josh's response. But it never came.

Out of the corner of my eye, I watched my husband fall awkwardly on his side. *Did he just pass out?* Worry threw me into a fast sprint across the living room to the couch where Josh laid. When I grabbed his shoulders and flung him upright, everything I understood about life changed.

Michael, a speaker that I often listen to from the CouncilOfTime website broadcasts once said, "Fear is unfounded truth gone wild inside of your head." That statement would hold true, looking back over most of my years. I worried about things that could potentially happen, with no evidence or cause to believe that those things actually *will happen*.

The type of ideas that drove my fear, (things like car accidents), seemed possible. But it was the absolutely *impossible* that would teach me the true essence of fear.

A few minutes before midnight on my husband's 39th birthday, March 24, 2016, - in one single moment, my entire reality shifted into the unthinkable. I fell into a place so dark, the air was too heavy to breath - a type of terror that I never before knew existed.

I *thought* I knew fear before that moment. I *thought* I was strong and brave - calculated in managing my life in a way that limited or even removed the opportunity for destruction in our lives. I was the woman that planned everything life could potentially throw in my direction. I was the hard-working, over-protective, problem solving mother and wife that would do anything to keep my family out of harms way. But all the protection in the world couldn't stop the impossible that happened right before my eyes as I saw my husband go down.

At first glance of Josh's rearranged face, the air was violently and completely sucked out of my lungs. I couldn't think. I couldn't speak. I couldn't even breath. And in response to the most devastatingly awful sight I'd ever seen, I ran. I don't mean like a quick jump backward in temporary shock. I mean that I literally stretched out my legs and ran as fast as I could away from the scene - like a little girl caught in a nightmare, sprinting with every bit of strength I had - trying desperately to escape the horror that consumed me so completely.

In the book of 2nd Corinthians, (5:7), the Bible says "We walk by faith, not by sight." I once thought this scripture explained the battle that I struggled with inside of my head - fighting against visions of horrible things that could potentially happen to one of my loved ones. But sight doesn't take place in our imaginations - sight is physical. Sight is the manifestation of fear, witnessed before our own eyes. And in this moment, as my worst fear became a reality, the evidence of my faith was nowhere to be found. I was horrified.

I don't remember much about the drive, following the ambulance to our local emergency room. I vaguely remembered family members arriving and the conversations taking place with medical staff. I only remember my fear.

My mother took turns hugging the kids as I prayed over Josh's body - laid out on the stretcher in the ER of Kingwood Medical Center. My prayers were nothing like the instructions found in the book of James (1:6):

*"But let him ask in faith, nothing wavering. For he that wavereth is like a wave of the sea driven with the wind and tossed away."*

My prayers were short, empty and definitely wavering - like desperate cries I made with my mouth, while inside wondering: *Where is God? He's not here! He's not watching! He's not doing anything to help us!*

The terror and anguish on the faces of my children was more than I could bear - almost as horrid as the image of Josh's face - lifeless and disabled by the immediate effects of a massive brain stroke.

We were told that the clot busting drug would likely have Josh back to normal within a few hours. But the good news brought me no peace. It's as if I didn't hear the doctors and their predictions because while Josh

15

was undergoing treatment, I was planning next steps - obsessed with one thing and one thing only - getting Josh moved to a better hospital.

I stayed busy making phone calls to anyone and everyone that I knew who had connections in the med center. I called and left messages, then hung up and called back again - frantically trying to wake people up from their sleep, as it was now into Friday morning.

"I know you're sleeping and I'm sorry to wake you. But if you get this message, please help me. Josh is in trouble and I need to get him transferred downtown." I spoke into the voicemail of our friend Neha. Josh had coached her son Kaleb throughout our years in little league football. I remembered that she had a number of family members who worked in the med center downtown.

I don't exactly know why I worked so hard that night to get him transferred, especially considering that we were told by the medical staff that Josh would likely be fine following the clot busting treatment.

Maybe I was following an inner voice of instruction. Or maybe I was still trying to control my fear - searching for a solution - something that I could do to end the nightmare.

I learned that a person in shock has limited abilities to do anything productive - especially in making decisions. I could only process a small bit of information. Seeing a big picture was impossible. Instead of looking for an outcome of 3 months from now or even 3 days from now, I was focused on 3 minutes from now - battling just to get through every passing moment.

Around 9 in the morning, a lady approached me in the waiting room and said that I could bring one family member with me to visit Josh in ICU. Josh Jr. wanted to come along. A few minutes later my mother snuck in the room to join us.

Josh was awake, but extremely groggy, and he seemed to be in a lot of pain. A doctor joined us to discuss Josh's status. He explained that Josh had suffered a massive stroke and the clot busting treatment hadn't worked as they had hoped.

He told us that they had identified the clot in his neck - caused by a dissected carotid artery, a major artery that carried blood to Josh's brain had broken. And as a result, the body tried to form a scab over the break and had developed a large clot that closed off the artery.

The doctor suggested a procedure to go in to Josh's artery and remove the clot. But it was risky because they could potentially break the clot lose and send it into Josh's brain, causing another major stroke.

I don't recall the questions I asked but I know that my focus was heavily on Josh's current state - he wasn't moving the left side of his body, he wasn't talking - he seemed to barely even be alive.

"Well at this point the damage is already done." The doctor said to me.

"What do you mean? He can't get better?"

"No, Mrs. Manfred. We can try to remove the clot as a measure to prevent a second stroke. Maybe we can save his life, I'm not sure. But the condition of your husband will not improve either way. There's nothing we can do about the damage to his brain. It is irreversible."

I felt a voice inside of me strongly disagree with the doctors words - as if I was throwing them into the wind. *Lies! He's just a suburb doctor. He doesn't know what he's talking about!*

At that moment, I realized that my son was now in a full blown cry - shaking and screaming hysterically.

"Why would you say such a thing in front of my kid?" I asked the doctor, with tears so heavily flowing I could hardly speak.

"Do you want us to do the procedure or not?" He asked with an emotionless expression.

"Doctor my husband is 39. He's not 80! There has to be something we can do to fix this!"

17

"We can try to stop the clot from causing more damage. That is all we can do. Yes or no Mrs. Manfred?"

"No. I want him out of this hospital and in care of doctors who can help him!"

I immediately went back to trying to control the situation, following the only solution I could think of. I picked up my phone and began texting everyone who had been making phone calls for me in attempt to get Josh transferred. One of my friends I'd texted, told me that I would need to speak with the head nurse to request the transfer and release of Josh.

After about half an hour, a short woman with brown hair entered Josh's room.

"You asked to speak to me? I'm Susan, the head nurse."

I explained to Susan that I wanted Josh transferred to the med center right away. She cut me off mid-sentence, "Miss Manfred we can't release Josh for a transfer."

She said the best she could do was request a hearing on Monday in the administrative meeting - and at that time, the hospital board may decide to release Josh.

"We don't have until Monday. He's laying here dying and your hospital is doing nothing to help him! He's *my* husband. I can take him to another hospital if I want to," I argued.

"You would have to put him in your car and drive him there, and he's not stable enough to survive the drive. That's your only option. I can't approve a transfer because we've already accepted care of him."

I couldn't believe my ears. How can a hospital hold my husband hostage, against my will? At that very moment, a young man interrupted our conversation and asked, "Are you Miss Manfred?"

"Yes, I am."

He held up an iPad toward my chest. "Can you sign here please? We forgot to get your signature last night to accept care of your husband." *Wow! What are the odds of that happening?*

I smiled at Susan and said. "Well, I guess you have to let me transfer him because I'm not signing anything." She nodded with an annoyed look on her face and disappeared around the corner.

Within the hour, Susan returned to inform me that an ambulance had been ordered to pick up Josh and transfer him to a hospital in the med center. And by 5 o'clock, I was loading the kids in the car to follow the ambulance downtown.

---

**Facebook Post:**

Josh Had a major stroke last night. We are waiting on transfer to Hermann in the medical center. I need God to keep his hands on this family through this and bring him out of this. Please lift him up in your prayers.

---

On the drive to downtown following the ambulance, I felt a sense of victory inside of me. I had made it through the worst night of my entire life. Not only had I faced my worst fear, but I had also overcame the dreadful hospital, the emotionless doctors and the stubborn administrators who had refused to let us leave Kingwood Medical.

I knew Josh's condition was still serious but I also felt strongly that we were now on the path to resolving our crisis. I thought back over the last countless hours spent searching for a way to get Josh transferred to the med center, and everything that had fallen into place. Neha had been such a blessing for us in pulling strings and contacting her father-in-law at the med center hospital to help get Josh accepted into a room. Then there was the situation with the hospital forgetting to get my signature - allowing us to transfer him.

It was truly amazing the way the pieces just seemed to fall into place perfectly. And somewhere inside of me, I felt a sense of pride that I had been able to maneuver through all of those obstacles. Despite the overwhelming presence of fear, panic and shock that consumed me, I had been able to make the right decisions for Josh. *Josh is going to be fine,* I thought to myself. *And he's going to be so proud that his brave wife overcame these horrid obstacles and fought for him,* I boasted in my thoughts.

## *Afterthoughts....*

I'd spent much of my adult life planning for the unthinkable - captivated by fear. But when true fear reared its ugly head, I had managed to somehow face it. Even within the most adverse circumstances, I had found the power and the strength to keep a glimpse of sanity over the last 24 hours. But was I really overcoming anything, or was strength just a figment of my imagination, based on loss not yet seen?

In the book of Hebrews, bondage is described as "fear of death." Verse 2:15 says that Jesus defeated this for us; *And deliver them who through fear of death were all their lifetime subject to bondage, (Hebrews 2:15).* Fear of death was the bondage that ruled my life every waking moment - not for myself but for my loved ones. Josh was alive and therefore I was alive - yet still holding onto hope that death would not be the outcome of our crisis. And that's not conquering fear at all - instead its grasping at an illusion that what *I want* will ultimately come to pass.

In truth, the one thing that I was holding onto was the fact that Josh's heart was still beating - and for him, I would fight with everything I had to keep it that way.

Later in our journey, those on the scene would marvel at my *superwoman sense of strength* and collectiveness that I projected to others, for the sake of my kids. My mother would make comments like, "I have no idea how you remained so calm, Jodi." But later in our journey, I would learn the truth of that projected strength - that it had absolutely nothing to do with me.

# Chapter Two

# *Room* 79

## Entering the Valley

My daughter called me just as we were about to pull into the hospital. She was riding in the ambulance with Josh and the paramedics.

"Mom, they said you can't follow them to the ambulance entrance. You'll have to park and meet us at his room."

"Ok, where do I go?"

"He'll be on the 7th floor in room 79." She replied.

"Ok Baby. I'll see you up there in a few."

The hospital was enormous and highly confusing. I parked on the 3rd floor of the parking garage and walked fast trying to follow signs, stopping a few times along the way to ask for directions as we walked long halls of green tiles to different intersections inside.

Once we got up to the Nuero ICU floor, a lady behind a desk greeted us and called for a nurse to show us floor procedures. The nurse demonstrated how we must wash our hands and put gloves on each time we enter through the double doors. We also were required to wear room number badges, and only 2 visitors would be allowed in his room at one time.

I was excited to learn that the hospital allowed us in and out anytime we wanted - Kingwood hadn't allowed anyone into ICU unless it was visiting hours. And as far as floor procedures, they had none.

Josh had two nurses assigned to him. They were both polite as they worked to get him hooked up to all of the noisy machines, explaining each step of the procedures to us all. I was relieved to see so much attention on Josh from his new care staff.

We stepped out for a few minutes while they ran tests and scans on Josh. Tj, his male nurse said that Josh was doing really well. He explained that they would watch him closely over the next few hours, and hopefully Josh would be allowed to check out of ICU into a regular room by morning.

The medical staff was a breath of fresh air compared to the place we'd left and I felt confident that Josh was in care of the best doctors, best nurses and with one of the highest rated brain science teams in the entire nation.

Shortly after we arrived, Josh's new staff stopped in to perform another check-up and scan on Josh. This time, the doctors stayed in the room for an extended period before we were invited back in.

The stroke experts walked us through images of Josh's clot located in his carotid artery and delivered to us their plan of action. They would go in with a tiny camera and attempt to remove the clot, if possible. It was the same procedure that the doctor at Kingwood Medical had discussed with me. But this time, I said "yes". I had a high level of confidence in the new staff treating Josh. And I believed that they would be able to get rid of the clot that was lingering over Josh's life - like a time bomb waiting to go off.

**Facebook Post:**

They are preparing Josh for a procedure to go into the arteries in the brain and find/fix the blockage. Praying they find it, fix it and we start turning around here toward recovery. They are coming to take him shortly.. please continue to help me pray.

About an hour later we were allowed to return to Josh's room. He was sleeping. The doctors joined us and explained that the procedure was not successful.

Apparently, his clot was too much of a risk to try and operate on. Bad news loomed over his ICU room as they explained a solution that wasn't a solution at all. Josh would be given high doses of blood thinners to try and prevent the clot from busting loose and destroying the rest of his brain.

"Then what happens after that?" I asked - sure that there was a light at the end of the tunnel, as a future plan to resolving the issue.

"Our hope is that the blood thinners can keep it from dislodging and perhaps it can resolve over time." The doctor answered.

So, basically, Josh had a clot that couldn't be removed and would potentially take his life at any moment. The doctors were relying upon medicines to stabilize it. But there was a chance that it would never go away - a 24/7 death sentence lingering over his life from this point forward.

I tried to digest the conversation, but couldn't. *There had to be another way,* I told myself. For the time being, I was optimistic in that he was still in care of the best doctors possible. And when the opportunity surfaced, I believed they would be able to resolve the clot issue somehow.

---

**Facebook Post:**

Yesterday was the worst day I've had in all my years here on Earth. I experienced things I'd hoped I'd never have to see. The enemy viscously attacked my family, on a day we should've been celebrating Josh's birthday and his life. But, he's attacking the wrong woman. He hasn't rattled my faith, if anything he's given us all a reason to strengthen our bond with God and with one another. Josh is talking to me this morning. He knows what's going on, he also knows where he's at. He's asking about what happened. He's asking about the kids and telling me he wants to go home and take a bubble bath. I'm crying tears of joy at the thought of that day, when he's healed and I get to take him back home. He grabbed my hand while ago and said to me "tell them to get the demons out of here", pointing at the side of his brain. He held my hand and I prayed over him, and I could see him nodding to my words. He knows what he's fighting against and I believe Josh will win this battle. Right now they're starting him on another medicine to thin the blood and try to reduce the clot. Please help me continue to pray for him.

---

About an hour later, they ran scans on Josh again - it was part of the ICU procedures and since Josh was at risk of brain swelling, they had to run frequent scans to keep an eye out for any changes.

A short man in a white coat pulled up images and began to speak to me and my mother, pointing out dark and light areas in a circular image that I couldn't comprehend. But even though I didn't understand the diagram of Josh's brain, I understood the word "surgery," and my heart instantly fell to the bottom of my stomach.

The doctor explained that Josh's brain was swelling rapidly and that they would need to cut out a portion of his skull, in order to allow room for his brain to swell out.

"When do you need to know?" I asked, assuming we had time to think through our options.

"We have to take him into surgery right now. Mrs. Manfred it's the only option Josh has to survive."

I nodded and stepped away as the team of doctors worked quickly around Josh's hospital bed. His mother, Vivian stayed by his side holding his hand and giving him words of encouragement.

*How did we go from stabilizing a blood clot to life-saving, emergency brain surgery?* I wondered, as thoughts raced inside of my mind. The familiar sense of shock that had overtaken me in our living room, as I had watched Josh collapse in front of my eyes, was trying to return to me again.  I was terrified by the long words and extensive lists of complications that the doctors called out.  The room was closing in on me and I worried that I would simply pass out at any moment.

"Jodi? Jodi where are you?" Josh muttered.

"Im here baby."  I answered as I approached his bedside and wrapped my fingers around his forearm.

"Is it a good doctor Jodi?"  I pulled knowledge from a voice deep inside of me, knowing absolutely nothing about the man who was about to take a saw to my precious husband's head.

"Yes baby.  You're in care of the best surgeons in Houston," I whispered, trying my hardest to hide the fear that was evident in my quivering vocal chords.

Family members crowded around Josh's bed like a chorus of encouraging phrases, adding to my attempt at easing Josh's worry.

"Jodi?"  Josh twisted his neck searching the many faces at his bedside to find my eyes.

"I'm still here Josh."

"Are you sure we should do this?"  The nervousness in Josh's broken expression sent a chill up my spine as I fought away terrifying visuals of what was about to happen to the space behind Josh's beautiful brown eyes.  I wanted to scream, *No! I 'm not sure about anything! Why is this is happening to us!*  And even in my fear, I was absent understanding - struggling to grasp what was actually taking place.

That dreamlike state of thinking *this can't be real*, was becoming commonplace for me.  Maybe it was my body's way of dealing with things that can't be dealt with in attempting to processing thought logically.  Nothing was logical in my world at that moment.  The impossible had happened and the nightmare continued.

I leaned down and softly kissed Josh on the top of his hand, "Baby we have no choice.  I love you." I told him.

Within a matter of seconds, the staff was wheeling Josh's bed out of his ICU room - Josh lifting his only arm that still had feeling, straight up in the air, forming a thumbs up gesture as he disappeared down the hallway, through large metal double doors.

Something about the confident yet odd gesture, coming from a man who was heading into life-saving brain surgery, provided me a sense of strength for a short moment. And once again, I reminded myself that Josh was in care of the best of the best - *these surgeons would fix this for us and we'd be home in no time,* I tried to convince myself.

**Facebook Post:**

———————

I have never had my faith tested the way it's being tested at this moment. I have given my fear and my worry to God and We are ready to receive this miracle. Amen.

———————

I battled fear with a sense of logic that the world had taught me. Science was advanced. Solutions were always obtainable. Probable outcomes were based on training and preparation. And I repeated the words inside of my mind that I'd delivered to Josh moments before - *You're in care of the best surgeons in Houston.* I prayed, but I was the double-minded man, *(James 1:8)* - believing that God would spare Josh's life, while putting half of my faith in the doctors, (the worldly experts of our crisis.)

I talked back and forth with my mom, Josh's mom and our children - trading words of encouragement and half-truths of what was happening with the kids.

I might well have been in that operating room with Josh, knocked out with anesthesia, because nothing around me was real. My body was going through motions on autopilot - smiling and nodding. But I was missing. My thoughts. My heart. Everything inside of me was curled up in a a little ball of intense stress, willing the man that I love to make it through this procedure.

More than 5 hours had passed, as my mother, Lil Josh and Kenna were my only company left in Josh's empty hospital room. My mother offered to get the kids a bite to eat. It was a good idea, but not one I was capable of thinking up. Eating, drinking, sleeping - even breathing seemed foreign and forgotten in my troubled state of mind.

I paced back and forth in the small square room, unsure if I would just pass out cold from my worrying, if they didn't give me an update on the surgery soon.

After my mom and the kids disappeared around the corner to try to find some food, I jumped on my cell phone and posted an update on social media - asking for friends and associates to pray for Josh's surgery. I prayed too, remembering a scripture I'd recently learned in the book of Mark.

*Therefore I tell you, whatever you ask for in prayer, believe that you have received it, and it will be yours, (Mark 11:24, NIV)*

In the weakest of my moments I didn't know how to believe that I would receive what I wanted. I wanted Josh to come out of that surgery talking and walking and moving the left side of his body. I wanted to believe that this was all just a dream that I'd soon wake up from. But reality and hope seemed far apart as I curled into a ball on the floor and did the only thing I knew how to do - I cried.

My silent prayers were interrupted by the sound of high heels clicking towards the door of room #79. I looked up and spotted a tall dark-skinned woman, immediately feeling relief at the sight of her smiling, familiar face. It was Blessing, (yes, that's her name).

Blessing was mother to one of our son's best friends at school. Daniel played receiver on Josh Jr.'s football team and also played 7on7 for the team Josh had coached over the summer. But, I didn't know his

28

mother very well until a few months back, when she showed up at our door to pray with me.

I didn't understand the purpose of Blessing's intrusion in our home at the time. And if I'm being honest, I was a bit offended when the smiling woman asked me "Do you know Jesus Christ as your Lord and Savior?" I'll never fully understand why that question rubbed me the wrong way. Perhaps I just assumed that people should know I'm a believer in Jesus Christ. Or maybe, I felt like a person's faith was off limits for questioning - like an intimate part of me that was none of her business.

Blessing had spoken scriptures to me that night, while we visited on my back patio. Then she confirmed a routine with me, ordering that we would fast together and talk at 10 pm twice a week, on Tuesdays and Thursdays. I nodded like I had no choice in the matter. And even today it's a mystery to me why my aggressive personality had left me that night in the presence of Blessing. I passively went along with what she suggested, then almost immediately asked myself, "What did I just get myself into" after seeing her out the door.

Blessing's bi-weekly prayer sessions and bible studies were somewhat confusing for me. She spoke quickly, spitting out scriptures and claiming healing over my family's lives in her deep Nigerian accent.

Normally, when I took her phone calls I would sneak into our spare bedroom and shut the door to find a place quiet enough to focus on what she was saying. Each time we spoke, understanding her accent became a little easier. And before long, I was beginning to fully understand her speech during our bible study/prayer sessions, although I wasn't sure that I was actually understanding much of it's meaning in my life.

Blessing chose scriptures of healing and faith each time we spoke. The bible had always been confusing to me - and learning about God's promises to heal the broken just felt like someone else's needs - not my own.

"The Lord is telling me to give you this scripture tonight," Blessing always gave this introduction before we began bible studies. She said that the Lord led her into my life and told her to teach me and pray with me. I wasn't sure if I believed the Lord worked like that - speaking instruction over my life to a woman I hardly knew.

But now, thinking back over our months in prayer together, her intrusion into my life to minister to me seemed almost like a miracle - *I believed God did send her to me.* She had no idea Josh would soon suffer a massive stroke. But God did. And he'd sent Blessing to prepare me for this crisis.

Blessing's presence as she entered Josh's empty ICU room was like a sword slicing through the heaviness in the air. I was so glad to see her - a woman of such strong faith and with a gift for delivering powerful prayer. She hugged me tightly and rocked side to side as I wept on her shoulder. Who knew a woman I'd only known for a few months could bring so much comfort to me in one of the darkest nights of my entire life?

I gave Blessing the quick explanation of what had happened. "Josh went into emergency brain surgery. I'm waiting on him to get out. He's been in there forever it seems, and I'm really nervous," I confessed.

Blessing smiled and rejoiced, praising the Lord as she stepped toward me, grabbed my hands in hers and began praying out-loud. She spoke scriptures of healing and thanked God for performing his promises over Josh's life. When her prayer was finished, she nodded at me confidently, with a huge smile on her face and said, "Josh is OK."

Just at that very moment, one of the doctors walked up behind me. He spoke quickly and said little. "Mrs. Manfred, Josh is out of surgery. Everything went fine. He's now in recovery and they'll bring him back here to the room probably within the hour."

My mom and the kids had perfect timing - arriving back to Josh's room as the doctor delivered the good news. It was a glorious moment of celebration as we all gathered and took turns hugging one another. I cried out to God with a tremendous feeling of relief upon my heart - smiling through waterfalls of tears that streamed from my eyes like an open faucet.

Blessing and Daniel decided to leave us after we received the good news. But as she was walking out, she turned back and signaled for me to step out of the room with her. Her expression was stern and serious.

"Jodi. This is not over. The enemy is about to attack." She whispered mysteriously.

I stepped back and stared into her dark brown eyes. She was gone before I could digest her startling warning. So, I did my best to shrug it off and went back to celebrating Josh's victory over the horrid brain surgery.

---

**Facebook Post:**

Surgeon just came and talked to us. Josh is out of surgery and surgeon said it went well. Thank you God and thank you everyone who has called, texted, posted and raised Josh's name into the mission of God's Angels on Earth through prayer. God has heard our prayers and continues to deliver on his word and his promise. We aren't out of ICU and we have a long way to go, no doubt.. But, we are blessed to have this wonderful man in our lives and we know he is headed to recovery and we will be bringing him home soon. The power of God is amazing. I have felt His strength when awful news was delivered to me, but I refused to believe the devil's tricks. Please keep praying we will get him home!

---

About 45 minutes had passed before they wheeled a sleeping Josh back into ICU Room #79. I was so happy to see his face, I didn't even pay attention to all the changes at first. After his bed was positioned, they quickly began transferring chords and tubes into the machines stationed against the wall.

The kids took turns trying to talk to him. He was unresponsive and I explained that it was because the anesthesia hadn't yet worn off. I hoped that was the reason, anyway. They were overjoyed just to hold his hand and whisper in his ear, "I love you dad."

---

**Facebook Post:**

*He performs wonders that cannot be fathomed, miracles that cannot be counted, (Job 5:9, NIV,)...* The kids were able to see Josh for a few minutes when he finally got back from surgery. They took him at 5:45 and didn't bring him back to ICU until 11:30pm. But he's back and he's being very strong... And so are the kids. I know it's hard for them to see him like this - it's hard for me too. He's their rock - the strong, loving father that's always there to protect them and make them feel secure. He's squeezing my hand and he says "love you" but otherwise he's sleeping deeply - still very drowsy from surgery. Now that the swelling in the brain has been addressed, the next challenge is the clot. I'm praying that the Lord pulls it out at the root and gets it out of his body! In Jesus Name, Amen.

---

With everyone's anticipation at ease following the news that Josh had made it through the surgery, my mom thought it would be a good idea to take the kids to get a few hours of sleep. My step-brother and his wife own a furnished apartment business in the medical center and had been so kind to set up a free room for us, just a few blocks away from the hospital. Josh and I weren't all that close to Sean and Candice - in fact we had only met them a few times before. I was surprised and very grateful to learn that they were helping us in providing such a nice gift that couldn't have been more needed, considering our home was nearly an hour away.

I hugged the kids and thanked my mother for taking care of them for me while I stayed with Josh. She tried to talk me into going with them -

as she studied me with worry written on her face. "Why don't you just lay down for an hour or two and then I can drive you back up here," she insisted.

I knew I looked bad. I hadn't slept in over 48 hours. But I wasn't going anywhere - not until Josh was ready to go home with me.

Once the nurses were finished working at his bedside, I was left alone with him. His face was swollen and he wore large gauzes, taped over the side of his head. A tube connected to the area above the back of Josh's neck, pouring a steady stream of blood into a large container that was attached to the side of his hospital bed. He looked so broken - so invaded. It was hard to grasp that my beautiful, athletic, strong and healthy husband had just went through major brain surgery.

I cried over him with so much hurt inside of me, as I studied his lifeless body. "How could this happen to him?" I asked out loud - no one around to answer my aimless inquiries.

**Facebook Post:**

My best friend from middle school just sent me this verse. Thank you Kari, this scripture is truth.

*(Psalms 66:17-20, NIV): I cried to him with my mouth, and high praise was on my tongue. If I had cherished iniquity in my heart, the Lord would not have listened. But truly God has listened; he has attended to the voice of my prayer. Blessed be God, because he has not rejected my prayer or removed his steadfast love from me.*

God is LOVE and he loves Josh so much. He loves Josh as I do and as our children do. He will heal him. Thank you all so much for the prayers and support. Please keep praying - All of us are God's children. He is listening to us. Have faith with me that HIS word and HIS miracle is done. We accept Josh's miracle and we thank God because we know he will do it.

-----------------

Around 5 in the morning, Josh's nurse, TJ stopped in to do his routine checks on Josh.  He tried to wake Josh and get a response - delivering the same questions that the nurses asked each time before.  "Can you tell me your name?  Do you know where you are are?  Do you know why you're here?  Can you tell me your wife's name?  Do you know who the president is?

Josh had struggled to answer these questions before.  But this time, he didn't even make an attempt.  "Josh I need you to wake up.  Can you hear my voice Josh?  Can you nod your head for me?"  TJ shook Josh's arm as he spoke loudly over Josh.  Then he stepped away and picked up a phone that was installed against the wall in Josh's room.

"Jodi?"  TJ laid the phone back on the receiver after several minutes of discussion with whoever was on the other end of the line, and then he approached me with a kind smile on his face.  "I'm going to need you to step outside for just a few minutes , OK?

Terror ignited in my veins as I sensed the worry in TJ's eyes.

"Why what's happening TJ?  Is Josh OK?"

TJ laid strong hands on my shoulders and moved me against a chair, signaling for me to sit down.

"I think so.  But his pupil isn't responding to light, so we have to do a few scans just to make sure everything is fine," he lied to me - as I would later learn.  When the pupil doesn't respond to light, its very bad news.

I paced down the hall as I watched a team of doctors rush into Josh's room - some pushing large machines (mobile brain scan devices).  Praying for the best, I stood still, reminding myself to breathe as a tall man wearing a surgeon's cap approached me.

"Mrs. Manfred, I need to speak with you about your husband, and I'm sorry but I don't have much time. " I nodded as the doctor continued.

"His brain is bleeding and the swelling is also increasing very quickly. We must remove another piece of his skull, cut out his temporal muscle and extract a part of his brain. I need you to sign here," He held up a black screened device with a signature line.

"Is he going to be OK?" I asked - desperation trembling in my voice.

"Well, honestly I don't know the answer to that. This is very rare for us to have to go back in and do this procedure. Mrs. Manfred, your husband's chances of surviving this surgery are not favorable."

I would later read the meaning of "not favorable," was defined in terrifyingly high mortality rates in various brain studies that discussed swelling, (hemorrhage) and brain bleeds. Josh had *both*.

"We have to take him now. You have less than a minute if you want to say goodbye — if there's anything you want to say to your husband before we take him."

*Say goodbye?* The phrase punctured me like a thousand knives submerged in my chest. I couldn't comprehend such a thing. *What did I do wrong? I prayed constantly. I had fought the fight of faith for Josh! I went to extremes to get him in the best possible hospital with the best possible surgeons on hand. Didn't they save lives everyday? Why couldn't they save Josh's life? Why did this surgeon speak such awful things? Didn't they have hope? Was there such a thing as hope?*

I followed the surgeon back into room #79, feeling like a little girl that was being led to the edge of a cliff, where I would step off and never return again. *I couldn't lose him. I can't leave this hospital room without Josh! How could this be happening to us?*

As I held his hand and prayed harder than I'd ever prayed before - I searched his face for a response. *"Please wake up Josh and talk to me. Josh it's me. Please talk to me!"* I pleaded to his motionless swollen eyelids. He didn't respond.

"God, please don't take him!" I muttered out loud. As bad as Josh's broken body had looked since the stroke, he had at least kept consciousness. The evidence of his life - his battle to keep life, was found in his ability to move a finger or open his eyes, or at least attempt to talk to me. But that was gone now. Josh had went to a place where he couldn't hear me anymore, and that wasn't something I could handle.

One of the doctors yelled out across the room, "Someone grab her! Get the priest in here!" I don't know if I was in the process of fainting. Or if there was another reason he instructed the nurse to grab me. I didn't know anything, but I heard a voice inside of me at that moment, shake every cell inside of my body as it shouted, "Satan is a liar!"

"No, we're good. I don't need a priest! Josh is going to live!" I claimed - staring the doctor straight in the eyes with a brief sense of courage inside of me. It came and left again as quickly as it had arrived.

"Miss Jodi, can I pray with you?" A tall, muscular black man with long dreads pouring out from under his surgeon's cap grabbed hold of my hands.
"Yes," I whimpered.

I later learned that this man of God was the anesthesiologist that would control Josh's blood pressure, monitor his blood loss and manage his vital signs, among other responsibilities through the surgery.

After he prayed with me hand in hand, he placed a blue glove under my chin and raised my eyes to meet his. "Listen to me. God is in control." I nodded in agreement.

"It's a miracle that your husband is even here right now. There are only a few surgeons in the entire state of Texas than can perform the surgery your husband needs at this moment. And one of those surgeons is standing right there." The man signaled, lifting a finger to point at a short man, reading a clipboard, dressed in a white coat.

"You give this to God and you believe with all of your heart that God will take care of him. You hear me?" Tears streamed down my face in waves of outpouring - like a dam had just been broken releasing massive amounts of water onto my cheeks.

"Ok..." I muttered through strained vocal chords, nodding my head.

The team of doctors left suddenly with Josh, leaving me to a silent and somber ICU room #79. I tried to walk to a small chair in the corner of the room, but my legs would no longer carry me. I was fading into a place of utter and complete helplessness.

After collapsing on the floor, I tried to crawl toward my purse - straining to lift fingers and pull my cell phone from the small black bag.

"Help me." I texted to my mother, before collapsing into the fetal position and closing my eyes tightly.

The adrenaline that had kept me going over the last few days, was no more. And the battle that I'd fought so vigorously was over. There was nothing I could do to save Josh now. There were no more decisions to make. There were no more words of encouragement to offer to my children, who had no idea that their father was walking through the valley of death at that very moment.

How could I have ever explained that to them, that their father might not ever come home? The best surgeons in the world had just told me to say goodbye to the man I'd loved since I was 15 years old. I had never felt so shattered in my entire life.

If Josh was going to die that morning, I was going to die with him. And within the darkest spaces of my defeated heart, I silently pleaded with the Lord to take me with him... to take me instead of him. To just take me out of my misery in this horrid, unthinkable nightmare!

Up to this this point, I'd done a good job convincing myself that I had faith. But faith in what? I prayed to the Lord and spoke his words and claimed healing over Josh's life. But I had also leaned on my own understanding - placing hope in skilled medical teams, award winning hospitals and top of the chain brain surgeons. They're just people - imperfect like you and me. They go to work and perform surgeries. Sometimes they're successful and sometimes they're not. They aren't miracle workers. They aren't God.

I had never felt so powerless in my entire life. My husband was facing his moment of truth - to live or to die. And I had absolutely no say in the matter. Josh belongs to God. He brought him into this world and he decides when to take him out of this world. My only hope was in God having mercy on our family.

I gave up. I mean, I *really* gave up. Laying on the cold floor of ICU Room #79, I surrendered everything I was to Jesus and begged him to take care of me. In the deepest parts of my soul, I gave up the fight and I handed Josh over to God and then prayed these 5 little worlds, *"Father please let him live....."*


### — Laying it Down at the Cross —
I don't know how much time had passed when my phone vibrated with a text message response from my mother, who was at the apartment with the kids.

*I can't come I'm having a vertigo attack. I'm sending MaeKenna to get you.*

The normal me would jump from the floor and call my mother in panic at the thought of my 15 year old, unlicensed daughter maneuvering behind the wheel of a vehicle through the confusing and overpopulated streets of the downtown med center. But the normal me was gone. I didn't care. I couldn't care because there was no strength inside of me to object to anything happening in the world outside - even the dangers of my little girl driving my big truck without assistance.

I closed my eyes tightly and tucked my chin underneath my chest - listening to the sound of my skull rubbing against the cold, hard hospital room floor. Then suddenly, I fell into a great peace…

> *I drifted off into a vision and felt the heaviness removed from my heart. I saw the sunlight peaking over the rooftop of my neighbors house as Josh's white truck pulled into our driveway. He jumped out and rounded the front bumper as my son approached him, then locked bodies with him in a heartfelt hug. Both men were dressed nicely, (my son and Josh). I wondered what the special occasion was. Could it be Josh Jr.'s graduation day? It had to be something big, I thought, as I studied the prideful expression on Josh's face. He embraced our grown-up looking son with such excitement. My heart smiled watching the two men talking and walking together.*

Then it ended. As quickly as the vision came, it disappeared, jolting me back into a sobering reality. But that moment of indescribable peace had been enough to dry my eyes temporarily. He'd heard me. He was there with me. Jesus was there in that room, I could feel him!

I felt hope, even though everything my senses could understand about what was happening to my life told a story of doom.

With the bit of strength this vision had placed into my broken little 5'2, 99lb. frame, I crawled to my knees, and then to my feet, and made my way down the hallway, through the double doors and to the elevator shaft.

The journey along this long walk to reach the outdoor area in front of Memorial Hermann was lost in my memory - another piece of the big blur that I'd not recall that day.

I sat on the curb and watched my black Yukon drive by, knowing I had to at least *try* to help my daughter find me. So I called her and did my best to explain to MaeKenna the road structures.

"You're on a one-way street and you just passed me." I whispered into the phone. "You're going to have to make three rights at the next few red lights to get back to the front of this building." I instructed her.

MaeKenna was calm and collective on the other end of the phone. And I knew that she knew I was too broken to help her find her way back to me.

"Don't worry Mom. I'm fine and I will find you. Just hang in there, I'm on my way." Tears of gratitude came to me as I realized how brave my little girl had been through all of this.

Here I was, not even able to get up and walk to the street corner. And, my mom was stuck in bed suffering with vertigo - which was induced by her high level of anxiety and lack of sleep. We were all falling apart at rapid speed. Yet my beautiful, brave daughter was somehow holding it together for all of us - our strength when we were weak.

It was a moment that would multiple into many, when I could feel the presence of Jesus working in us - one by one. It's like He was transferring his peace and power into different vessels. We took turns being strong for one another, when being strong was an impossible task.

I know it was the Lord that peeled me off of that ICU room floor and carried me down to meet my daughter that morning. I know it was the Lord that sent text messages to Josh's family as I rode passenger side with my MaeKenna on the short journey to the furnished apartment, my step-brother and his wife had set up for us. I know it was the Lord that had allowed me to reach the lowest point of my entire life - a place of utter and complete helplessness - stripping away everything, in order to show me *the only thing - Jesus.*

When I cried out with all of my heart "Father please let him live," I had nothing left of me inside. In that moment there were no more ideas or thoughts passing through my imagination. My mind was completely taken captive by the powerlessness of my existence before a God that controls *everything*. He showed me what it felt like to truly surrender to him. He taught me what faith looks like and he showed me how to give the battle over to him - how to *lay it down at the cross*.

I know it was also the Lord that had worked through Blessing to warn me of the attack that she couldn't possibly have known was coming. It was the Lord that spoke to me the words "Satan is a liar". It was the Lord that sent that young anesthesiologist to pray with me, delivering such wise and spirit filled words. And, it was the Lord that had given me that vision that I would hold onto with everything I had - that vision of Josh healed. His strength he had revealed, in my lowest moment of weakness.

*Concerning this thing I pleaded with the Lord three times that it might depart from me. 9 And He said to me, "My grace is sufficient for you, for My strength is made perfect in weakness." (2 Corinthians 12:8)*

41

*— Our last family photos that we had taken together before Josh's stroke was ironically, the four of us standing at the foot of the cross in front of our church. —*

Perhaps one of the most popular scriptures from the Bible is Psalms 23:4. David wrote...

*Yea, though I walk through the valley of the shadow of death, I will fear no evil: for thou art with me; thy rod and thy staff they comfort me.*

What I learned about the *valley of the shadow of death*, is that I am no David. I *thought* I knew what faith was - brought up from an early age in the church and taught the story of Jesus dying on the cross for me. But believing in Jesus wasn't evident in my life at all. In fact, the essence of my life was actually in contrary to evidence of Christ living in me.

David's faith in God was so strong, he faced Goliath knowing it was humanly impossible for him to defeat that giant by his own means. Nothing in this world could offer him even a chance of victory - and certainly not a little stone. David accomplished the impossible because he knew where true strength comes from - God.

Looking back over my life before Josh's stroke, I realized that I had never known true faith. I'd been raised in a world of philosophical belief systems and I'd not only drank the Kool-Aid, but I had become a proponent to self-made success. I believed that I could control my circumstances, my health, my job, my family's safety - everything. By my efforts in making smart decisions and working hard to piece together the puzzle of what I wanted my life to look like, I thought I had things all figured out.

In the valley, I learned that my thinking was not only flawed, but in opposition to faith. I didn't trust God with my life - instead I tried to control everything - I was ruled by fear. And in the valley, God showed me what it looked like to lay down my life at the cross of Jesus. He brought me to the moment of truth in understanding that HE IS GOD.... and HE runs *everything.*

# Chapter Three

# *He* Lived

## Conversations from Heaven

I vaguely remember reading that text message that sent me jumping from a deep sleep out of the bed and up to my feet.

"He lived!" I screamed. I remember the relief - almost like an expectation. Something had changed inside of me a few hours before on the floor of Josh's room. I believed God was with me. I *really* believed.

Much of that morning seems like a mist - a vapor of sorts. Some of my memories of what I did or said to others almost felt dreamlike. But they were real - even as unthinkable as it all may have been. They were purposed. They were life changing.

Tiffany's text message was candy to my eyes, but also contained information that I was not ready to think about. When I arrived back in the hospital, she repeated the words from the doctor - the words I rebuked with the wholeness of my spirit.

"He'll never walk again." She explained. "The doctor said he may never eat or talk again, either. But he did say there's a chance that Josh will still have some of his memory. He's going to need a lot of love."

I partially ignored Josh's sister - not to be inattentive to the importance of the doctor's reported news. But I wasn't ready to buy-in to such a report. At first thought, I said to myself, *I don't care how messed up he is. I'll take care of him and love him no matter what.*

But as the focus of my thoughts shifted to what Josh would want, I knew that a life plagued by severe disability would never work for him. Josh was far too in love with his active lifestyle to accept a future that confined him to a wheelchair. His second home away from work was the gym - he lifted weights and played basketball with a group of college kids nearly every night.  Plus, he was vain - and I don't say that in an ugly way.  But being fit and looking good was extremely important to Josh - it always had been.  A paralyzed Josh watching TV all day, unable to speak or eat by himself just wasn't a visual I could put together.  It was an impossible concept.

Like a little girl's teddy bear that brought comfort when in fear, I took myself back to the vision God had given me of Josh healed.  That was the report I wanted to believe in.  And frankly, I didn't care how much experience these neurosurgeons had, or how many statistics were stacked up against Josh.  I didn't even care if it was scientifically impossible for Josh to ever leave a wheelchair after having a portion of his brain removed - *they're just people with opinions,* I told myself.

I focused on what the Lord showed me.  And I know what I saw.  I was going to believe with all of my heart that God had given me that vision as a promise to what our future would one day hold.  *Josh will be healed!*

---

**Facebook Post:**
*Now he that has made us for the same thing is God, who also has given unto us the earnest of the Spirit. Therefore we are always confident, knowing that, while we are at home in the body, we are absent from the Lord:  For we walk by faith, not by sight. (2 Corinthians 5:5 - 5:7)*

Most of you are waking up to begin a normal day. You'll soon make decisions like what's for breakfast, or, how to respond to the lady who will cut you off in morning traffic.

But one day, your normal day could be disrupted by an attack of Satan. I want everyone who's reading Josh's story to realize that his story is your story too.  We are all God's children with our own special unique gifts.  We are all loved very much by our creator and our Lord. We were all saved by the sacrifice of Jesus Christ - his unconditional love for us that paid the highest price for our sins and for our healing --- for divine health .

That doesn't mean the enemy can't attack any of us any time. When that happens, we are challenged to walk by Faith, not by sight. That's exactly what me and my family are doing. We are thankful, we believe, and we are walking by FAITH, not by sight.

Please take a moment this morning to walk by Faith for Josh. Visualize his complete healing, which is the miracle we accept from our faithful, loving God and believe that His miracle is the only truth - for our God's Word says it is so. It is done. We thank you God for the miracle of healing that you have issued on Josh's body. In Jesus's Name. Amen.

---

My optimistic attitude was attacked instantly, entering Josh's ICU room. He looked destroyed. The swelling covering his head down to his neck was significant. His face was no longer recognizable and his body seemed almost like a rag doll - pumping up and down as a long tube pushed oxygen into his mouth. *He's on life support*, I thought as my mind began to race, searching for an explanation.

I'd heard stories about life support - horrible tales of those who never came off of the assisted device, employed to breathe for patients who couldn't breathe on their own.

"Why is he on life support?" I asked anxiously, staring at the nurse who was adjusting Josh's blankets over him.

"They had to make that decision during surgery."

Fear battled to creep its way back into my thoughts. *Why didn't they warn me that Josh would come out of surgery like this?* Then I remembered, the doctor had in fact, warned me of much worse. And he

46

had been wrong. *Josh lived! Against the odds and statistics that persuaded medical opinion - by the Grace of God alone, Josh lived.*

I reminded myself that it was a miracle Josh was even breathing - even if it was a machine doing all the work for his lungs.

I would've assumed that being thankful in the midst of such extreme circumstances would be an impossible task. But oddly, being thankful was like a solution that fed medicine to my soul. With every new shocking sight, I combated the overwhelming feelings of fear and loss by focusing on the blessings that God had provided us.

Was it horrifying to watch my husband's life sustained by an electronic device? Absolutely. But he was alive. I repeated that phrase over and over to myself, *He's alive! Josh lived! He's here and he's alive!* - rejoicing and thanking the Lord for his mercy and kindness.

*Let us therefore come boldly unto the throne of grace, that we may obtain mercy, and find grace to help in time of need.*
*- (Hebrews 4:16)*

Josh slept throughout most of that day. I didn't want to be a bother to him but I couldn't help myself from trying to communicate, periodically. I would lean over and whisper into his ear.

"Baby it's me. I'm here. Can you hear me? Josh if you can hear me please can you try to squeeze my hand? Please, baby squeeze my hand!" I was desperate for a response from Josh. But none came.

Over the next few hours, I felt almost in a trance - swaying from side to side as I lifted my hands and prayed over Josh. "By the stripes of Jesus you are healed." I confessed out loud, over and over again.

I took short breaks to cry, and then mustard up the strength to get back into prayer again. It was like I was in a war zone and I didn't understand why. I just did what my heart led me to keep doing. I prayed and I prayed and I prayed more.

**Facebook Post:**
Josh is fighting for us and everyone that knows this man knows how tough he is. Since I was just a kid, he's been my rock. He's my best friend. I know his story has purpose beyond this fight. We will keep lifting him up in prayer until he defeats this evil. It will be done, in Jesus Name. Amen.

Heartbreak was like my bipolar friend that changed back and forth with every passing hour. As soon as I thought I'd reached the end of my tears, I found a fresh new batch flowing down my face. Then I would take a break from crying and fall into a state of gratitude - thanking the Lord and praising his name.

It was hard to see Josh like that - hour upon hour with no change. And because he wasn't even attempting to wake and communicate with me, I wondered more and more about the news Tiffany had shared from the doctors. The spirit of fear was always there lurking - fighting to find a way back into my thoughts. *What if I never get the chance to speak to him again? What if he doesn't even remember me when he wakes up?*

I don't know how much time had passed when a doctor I hadn't seen before entered Josh's room. He looked over Josh briefly and then stepped outside to give instructions to Josh's nurse. She nodded and then looked directly at me - I assumed they were talking about me.

"Jodi, I'm going to need you to step out in just a few minutes. They're bringing in a crew to remove the breathing tubes."

"That's awesome! He's ready to come off life support!" I beamed, misunderstanding her news.

"Well we don't know that yet." She sounded as if she were trying to be careful in choosing her words. "When they remove the tubes it's best if you don't watch - it'll be a little painful for Josh. Also, they won't allow anyone in here, in case he doesn't breathe on his own." *In case he doesn't breathe? If he doesn't breath he doesn't live...* My thoughts tried to finish her sentence that had left me hanging.

"And what happens if he doesn't breathe?" I asked.

"Then they have to put the tube back in as quickly as possible." She answered - making it sound simple, I assumed in attempt to ease my fears.

I stepped out when the team arrived. But I stayed close enough to see what was happening (peaking around the corner, hoping no one saw me). They didn't allow visitors to walk the halls because of privacy reasons. ICU was like a a constant trauma scene - doctors shuffling in and out to wheel patients off to surgery.

And more often then not, those episodes of fast-moving care teams were followed by the arrival of housekeeping - tending to the rooms hours after patients disappeared into surgery. Nuero-ICU was the saddest place I'd ever seen in my entire life.

Death was like a cloud, constantly hovering over everyone that passed through that place - family members stumbled around in zombie-like movements, with tracks of tears painting their faces. It was a place of hopelessness and *goodbye forevers*. It was also a place of revelation and reflecting upon what was really important.... *Life*.

**Facebook Post:**

They are coming in now to try and remove the breathing machine. He will breathe on his own as this miracle of God's says it is so. Amen!

*So do not fear, for I am with you; do not be dismayed, for I am your God. I will strengthen you and help you; I will uphold you with my righteous right hand. (Isaiah 41:10, NIV)*

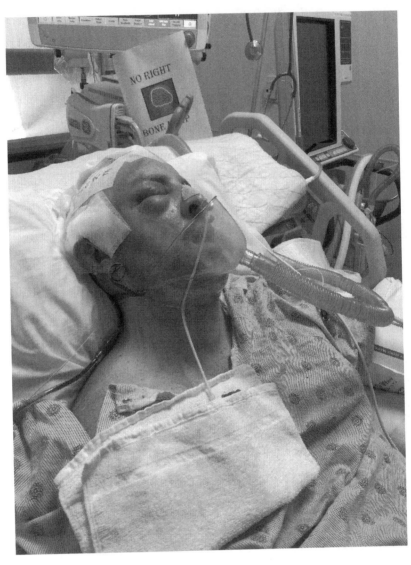

— *Josh in Nuero-ICU after he was taken off of life support* —

As the team appeared to be almost wrestling - making vigorous movements on each side of Josh's bed, I crept forward toward the doorway of his room - watching the action through a glass wall.

Stepping foot in the room at the exact moment the tube was ejected, I got to witness Josh taking his very first breath.

"Water!" He screeched - sounding like a forced whirlwind rushing out as a desperate whisper. His vocal chords were absent the effort, yet that one word that left his mouth, couldn't have been more clear.

He was breathing and he was awake! He was even attempting to speak! He said water! *Thank You Lord!*

---

**Facebook Post:**

He said "water!" As soon as the tube came out. Then he held his hand up and did the pinky thumb sign (his signal for "I need a drink".. If you've ever been to a restaurant with him you've seen the pinky-thumb gesture)...

Like 20 minutes in.. He's breathing on his own!!! It's stressful and he has a few hours of careful monitoring and battling to cough out the congestion, but right now he's doing a good job!

---

The nurses would sometimes join in with me in celebrating Josh's successes, but the doctors almost seemed annoyed by my optimism - constantly reminding me of the potential loss that lingered over my husband's life. They looked at me like I was some sort of crazy, mentally detached head case - in denial of my reality.

"Mrs. Manfred, you need to know that your husband is very, very sick. The first 3 days after this surgery are critical. We just don't know what will happen yet. He is not out of danger." A short tanned-skin man spoke in an Indian descent accent. He was one of the doctors on Josh's care team that stopped in twice a day to review scans and type notes into his rolling laptop.

Victories were like checkpoints in the ICU - keeping hope alive and faith elevated as the minutes passed by slowly. Physically speaking, Josh's room was far from a place of celebration - it was a terrifying setting. The sounds of machines over the sights of dried blood and monitors lighting up with alert messages was nerve racking, at best. Yet, the Lord gave me these little winks now and then to let me know that He was listening to my prayers - to let me know He had not left us.

As the minutes and hours ticked away, Josh was still paralyzed and still barely coherent. He wasn't talking or drinking or eating. In the short moments when he was awake, he seemed restless and agitated - reaching out with his right hand to grasp mine. I tried to comfort him and whisper words of encouragement. I prayed over him and told him I believed that the Lord would heal him.

Not being able to communicate was hard for Josh - and hard for me too. I wanted so badly to know what he was thinking. I wondered if he was in pain or if he was scared.

Repeatedly, Josh raised his hand and attempted to write letters with his index finger into the air. I focused so intently on his movements, trying to make out the letters. The nurses stuffed a pillow under his hand (as a canvas for his writing), then they gathered around to help us. Like a game of charades, we took turns blurting out words and then looking to Josh for confirmation of our guesses.

Finally, I got it! The thing he'd been trying to write on a pillow with his right index finger all day was *I LOVE YOU*. When I said the words out loud he nodded his head to tell me "yes," and then laid his head back in a sigh of relief.

Tears streamed from his eyes and I felt so heartbroken - understanding the unspoken message that stirred inside of my husband. I knew his pain was great, yet he didn't have a request or a complaint. In the most distressed time of his entire life, all he wanted to tell me was that he loved me. And without hearing him give an explanation, I knew deep down why this gesture was of such importance to him. Josh wasn't sure that he'd ever have the chance to tell me "I love you" again.

---

**Facebook Post:**
We met Julie a few hours ago, (his new nurse). She's been a blessing taking very good care of him after his rough night. He's finally comfortable and not asking for TJ anymore - TJ was his nurse before that took very good care of him.

Here's the bigger reason Julie is a blessing: she poked him in his left hand and got him to throw a huge elbow - not a little twitch, this was a UFC style blow. And he even held it up for a second before putting his arm back down!! Since Thursday night I haven't seen him move his left arm. Thank you God for sending Julie into this room to present another one of your amazing miracles.

He still has swelling.. he's running a fever.. he's still at risk for infection and other complications. We're still in the dreadful ICU. But, we're getting out of here soon! I know it!! This man has beaten every evil attack that has been thrown our way yet.

I'm laughing at you Satan. You are no match for my God and he has defeated you in the life of Josh Manfred. Josh is in the midst of a miracle. In Jesus name. Amen.

---

In walking with a loved one through the valley, prayer was no longer a chore that I had to remind myself to do before I went to sleep at night. Prayer became a life-line of what I had to do constantly. It was as natural and as vital as filling my lungs with air.

The Bible says in 1 Thessalonians: *Rejoice evermore. Pray without ceasing. In every thing give thanks: for this is the will of God in Christ Jesus concerning you. (Thes. 5:16-18)*

I don't know if what we did could be considered "rejoicing." But me, the kids and my mother locked hands around Josh's bedside as one unit, covering him with heartfelt love as we prayed together countless times throughout each day - crying tears of happiness and hope as we shared together in a belief that the Lord was hearing our cries. We spoke about scriptures and took turns studying the word of God, like it was an instruction manual to surviving our crisis.

---

**Facebook Post: *My Mom writes..***

The last 5 days have been a big blur and full of ups and downs. Watching my precious son in law and family going through the unimaginable is difficult to say the least but this event is also transforming lives all over. As I have sat in Josh's ICU room over the past several days I watch the kids at his bedside so unselfishly holding their dads hand, talking to him, telling them how much they love him and need him, and asking questions like "where does it hurt dad, give me a thumbs up dad" and then keeping a cool rag on his head.

But the greatest and most amazing thing is watching them grow in faith, believing in God, putting their hands on there dad and praying and reading him bible scriptures throughout the day. This evening this is my little grandson, Josh, laying on the floor beside his dad as he slept, reading the book of Jeremiah! Thank you God for all that you are doing for Josh, but also for many many others.

For my thoughts *are* not your thoughts, neither *are* your ways my ways, saith the Lord. For *as* the heavens are higher than the earth, so are my ways higher than your ways, and my thoughts than your thoughts. - *(Isaiah 55:8)*

---

*— Josh Jr. reading the book of Jeremiah, while laying on the floor of ICU Room #79 —*

Our temporary home in ICU room #79 had become our sanctuary - our alter - our place of praise. And while it wasn't as evident to me at the time, because my focus was solely on Josh's healing, our inner beings were changing in that room. Our desires were never so clear. We loved each other - without fault or conditions. We loved Josh. And the world that was spinning outside of those four walls where Josh fought for his life, just wasn't important to us anymore.

My kids would normally have been complaining that they were stuck in a hospital room instead of eating candy and hunting easter eggs. The holidays that passed by us in ICU were meaningless. Candy wasn't important. Love was all that mattered.

**My son wrote on Instagram:** *This year I don't want any Easter candy. I just want my dad back.*

When we weren't praying together or trying to communicate with Josh, I spent time researching scriptures from the Bible and reading our Facebook pages - which was full of encouraging thoughts and meaningful promises of our Lord.

I never thought such comfort could come from friends and associates who we hardly even spoke to. But in the valley, the power of others was real to me. I read through every last post, comment and message that we received. Hundreds of prayers and messages of encouragement poured in through our cell phones and social media pages. It brought me comfort to know that I wasn't screaming out to God on my own - that people from all over the world were lifting Josh up in prayer each day. I cried happy tears scanning through all of the supportive messages.

---

**Facebook Post: *Ken M. writes..***
Josh,
We all are praying for your health and strength bro. We spent many days coaching and yelling during our boys athletic childhood. I know God will take care of you and

your family. I know you love your family a whole lot and I need to hear you telling me stories about kicking butt!! I wish I could do more but Jodi is just as strong as you are. I spoke with Lil Josh and he will be strong too. MaeKenna will make sure Lil Josh is taken care of!! All of the guys are praying and staying strong!!!! Get up bro.... Let your faith lead you...we will smile about this and testify....God's will !!!!! #PrayforJoshManfred

---

**Facebook Post: *Sherra writes..***

As I read my morning devotional, these scriptures were the lesson: "The Potter formed it into another pot, shaping it as it seemed best to Him. (Jeremiah 18:4, NIV) He Who promised is faithful. (Hebrews 10:23, NIV) Consider that our present sufferings are not worth comparing with the glory that will be revealed in us. (Romans 8:18, NIV)

The One Who rolls the stars along speaks all the promises. Continue to hold on to His promises. Trust the untraceable ways of God and remember that these are but the outer fringe of His works. (Job 26:14) Jodi, He has already shown you. He has been at work preparing you for this. So, in His strong arms lay Josh down, so shall the work be done; for who can work so wondrously as the Almighty One!

---

I did my best to keep friends and family updated on Josh. It was the least I could do in return for all of the prayers and well wishes. I told mostly the good news - but then again, none of it probably appeared to be good news to those outside, looking in. And I was fine with that too.

It's strange that before Josh's stroke, I would never have dreamed I'd be on social media posting such horrific and intimate details of our lives.

I'd always thought that sharing my troubles with other people was a bad idea - a sign of weakness. But as we battled over Josh's bed in prayer, sharing our journey with others was just part of the process - like recruiting soldiers to help us on the battlefield.

I welcomed others to take the journey with us and connect with us through each day. I needed prayers and support and I greatly appreciated everyone who gave them. I believed in the power of prayer. And I challenged our friends, family and associates to join us in prayer as often as I could find time to post from my phone.

-------------------

**Facebook Post:**

God, thank you for providing the communities of people who have agreed with my heart's desire, my mind's focus and my Faith's request. Thank you God for hearing your children who come together in the name of the Lord - in your name, Father to worship you and to ask for the healing of Josh. Lord thank you for raising Josh up and forgiving his sins. Thank you for working this divine miracle that can only be by the power of YOU our Lord and Savior. In Jesus name. Amen.

I am overjoyed with love and compassion and gratitude for all the prayers we continue to receive for Josh. I love you all so much and I thank you from the bottom of my heart for believing in Jesus Christ our Savior and for following our merciful, righteous God by his Word, which is above all things! Thank you for walking with me by Faith, not by sight and for believing in the miracle we are asking of God. Your faith in God is the reason this miracle will be done.

*Is anyone among you sick? Let him call for the elders of the church, and let them pray over him, anointing him with oil in the name of the Lord. And the prayer of faith will save the sick, and the Lord will raise him up. And if he has committed sins, he will be forgiven. (James 5:14-15)*

---

Good news seemed to be little and bad news just kept coming our way. After the two brain surgeries, one of the staff's biggest concerns was infection. Just as I had began to get my hopes up that Josh would be stable enough to transfer out of ICU, his body revealed different plans.

---

**Facebook Post:**

Last night was challenging. Josh's temperature spiked, his swelling in his head became visibly increased and his blood pressure jumped through the roof. The nurse gave him different meds, with no success in calming him down. Finally the ICU doc appeared to check him out, at which point another immediate CT scan was ordered. My heart dropped at the familiar course of action and the fear of another surgery.

They gave him pain medicine (finally) to calm him for the scan. He relaxed a little.. Went to sleep and the neurosurgeon returned to let me know that all the new swelling is on the outside not the inside... Thank you God!

Since then the swelling has gone down much and he's sleeping peacefully right now. Thank you God for giving him the strength to defeat this challenge.

But he *was* wounded for our transgressions, *he was* bruised for our iniquities: the chastisement of our peace *was* upon him; and with his stripes we are healed. - *(Isaiah 53:5)*

---

Immediately following the scans and favorable results, Josh's blood work revealed that his body was now fighting infection.

I'd remembered the surgeons' warnings of how infection following brain surgery could be fatal. But in reminding myself of God's report - that vision of Josh healed, hugging our son in our front driveway - I knew the infection would not take Josh's life.

The nurses started him on antibiotics and Josh received a new doctor that specialized in infections - another white coat added to the 20 to 30 that were already assigned to his care.

I prayed my go-to prayer as the nurse administered the new meds in Josh's IV - "By the stripes of Jesus you are healed." And by the next day, Josh's fever had already broken. Not only that, but Josh woke up with a voice!

At first, the squeaky sound coming from Josh's lips was startling. He sounded a *little bit* like Josh. Perhaps it was what Josh may have sounded like before he hit the age of puberty.

Josh's voice was high-pitched and winded. It seemed as if he was laboring hard to create noise with his vocal chords. But, praise the Lord - he was now talking! It was our first *"Josh may never"* from the doctor's report that was now crossed off of the list - defeated by the blood of Jesus!

I couldn't seem to leave him alone with his renewed talent. I layered the questions as fast as my mind could put them together - so excited to be once again communicating with Josh: *How are you feeling? Does anything hurt? Baby, you're alive! Isn't that exciting? Josh, do you believe Jesus is healing you?*

I wasn't prepared for the answer Josh would deliver to that last question as he nodded and blurted out, "I know. I talked to him."

"You talked to who?" Josh didn't have a very good attention span. I had to ask him the question three times before getting more information from him.

"Jesus." He whispered.

"Josh you talked to Jesus? What did he say to you?" I pestered Josh to tell me more.

"He said I'm going to live." Josh was only able to stay awake for short periods of time. And with him exerting the massive amount of strength it took for him to now speak, his eyes were growing heavy quickly.

"Josh what else did he say?"

"I have to tell people." Josh muttered the incomplete thought.

"Tell them what Josh? What did Jesus say you needed to tell people?"

"Tell you later." Josh's whisper was the final string to his temporary coherence. He was fast asleep before I could drag anything more out of him.

I knew without a doubt in my mind that Josh had encountered the living God, because the idea that Jesus talks to people was something the old Josh just didn't believe in. Recalling a conversation we had a few months before Josh's stroke while laying in bed one night, I remembered Josh explaining his thoughts on how God works.

"You realize how many times the Bible has been tampered with over all these years?" Josh had asked me - setting up a debate that I wasn't willing to oppose. I too had questioned the reliability of the bible.
"Well I don't understand it. I've tried to read it so many times before - it's like reading a foreign language for me," I confessed. I told Josh that I felt like if God wanted me to know something, I wouldn't need to go read a book - he'd just tell me what he wanted me to know.
"You think he's just gonna talk to you?" Josh asked sarcastically as he let out a laugh. "You'll just be walking along minding your business and God will yell out through some trees, like, "Jodi, come

hither! We need to have a little chat!" He added, now fully making fun of me.

"Not like that obviously. But yeah, he's talked to me before." I felt embarrassed, attempting to defend something I was quite certain of, but wasn't brave enough to discuss.

"I don't believe all that stuff.. People on tv throw themselves on the ground and they're shaking and speaking gibberish *abadaaabeeeyahhh!*, claiming that God is telling this and telling them that. If God talks to people, we'd all hear him. So, obviously he doesn't talk to us." Josh concluded our talk that night.

But now, here we are just a few months later - the cynical man that I'd known for over 20 years lays broken in an ICU room. With his first day speaking, he confesses that he had talked to Jesus.

I thought about the voice that shook me as the doctors prepared to take him into his last surgery - *Satan is a liar,* it had said. And then the vision that brought a breathtaking sense of peace over me, after they'd wheeled Josh off. God had made his presence known to me. *How much more had he revealed of himself to Josh - the one who had literally been in the valley, fighting for his life?* I wondered.

---

**Facebook Post:**
But Jesus beheld [them], and said unto them, With men this is impossible; but with God all things are possible. *(Mathew 19:26)*

I feel the world changing today - slowing.... The feeling of suffocation that only God could relieve has constantly chased me around over the last six days. The enemy has tried many tricks and delivered many false testimonies but has been defeated repeatedly - unsuccessful and never a match for God's word and the promises that HE has delivered upon.

Many events of the day have brought a calmness into this room, an understanding. Some of these testimonies are beyond life changing and I can't wait for Josh to be able to share his miraculous story.

For me, I know Josh is still in ICU, and I understand what that technically is supposed to mean. But I know in my heart God has already moved him into the healing stages. I believe by this time tomorrow we will be posting from a different floor.

Lifting this man up with everything I've got until the day we bring him home…

---

It was a new day bringing new messages from Heaven. Josh was more alert and using his new speaking skill to demand things.

"Smoothie!" He screamed at the nurses. With one task down, (talking), Josh was now focused on the next thing he wanted back - his ability to drink and eat.

"Oh, I wish I could give you a smoothie but I can't. You could develop pneumonia Josh." The young, tall nurse explained to him.

A speech therapist had stopped in our room on the day before to assess Josh's swallowing ability, which apparently didn't go so well. She said that Josh's muscles in his throat weren't working properly. Therefore, liquid in his mouth would be taken to his lungs instead of his stomach.

Every time the nurses left his side, Josh would turn his attention my direction - begging me to get him a glass of water. I felt so guilty telling him "I can't", over and over again. I hated that he couldn't put any liquids in his mouth and his lips were visually beginning to peel from excessive dryness. But, I firmly denied him because I wasn't willing to risk Josh getting sick.

This also made it impossible for me to drink water - obviously I couldn't do such a thing in front of him. It would be cruel.

Every now and then while Josh was sleeping, I would sneak away to grab a bottle of water from the deli on the 1st floor. Eating wasn't something I had yet figured out how to do again. It's like the natural craving for food was completely removed from me. An entire week had passed without me intaking a single cracker.

When I would walk back from the elevator case, I always made it a point to glance through each of the rooms along my pathway to room 79. Most of the beds had turned over at least once already since we'd arrived. And while I hoped that the appearance of fresh sheets and clean trays meant a patient had graduated from ICU, I knew that wasn't the case for many of them.

I'd seen the teams of doctors swarming over patients as they rushed out to surgeries - exactly as I'd witnessed twice with Josh. And the sad reality was that many of them had never came back from those surgeries. Even more evidence was found in the faces of people gathered at all hours, outside in the waiting room. It was a room full of emotional distress - hugs, tears and occasionally even loud screams.

Nuero-ICU wasn't just any ICU - it was the place where the worst cases in all of Houston for brain injuries were sent. Most of the patients arrived here by life-flight throughout all hours of the night. I'd hear the commotion as teams worked to check-in new arrivals.

One room that I passed by each day seemed to not change. The adorable blonde headed little boy was maybe 11 or 12 years old, I guessed. He reminded me of my own son for some reason. I'd never seen him even move positions in that hospital bed, where he laid day and night under a breathing machine. Even more sad to me was the position of his mother at his bedside - also unchanged.

She never left him. Countless nights I'd walked that hallway, and every single time I glanced into his room, she was there sitting in that little chair next to his bed, holding his hand - weeping.

"You're not supposed to be wandering the hallways Miss Jodi." A familiar male voice startled me as I stood still, staring into the little boy's room.

"Tj! You scared me." I admitted.

"I'm just playing with you." He said, flashing a smile.

As I entered Josh's room, TJ followed behind me with his medicines for Josh in hand.

"Donor-cycle accident." TJ muttered quietly. I thought about his words - puzzled.

"What's a donor-cycle?"

"Motorcycle...." TJ raised his eyebrows playfully, poking fun at me for my lack of ability to put two simple words together.

"That's awful," I shook my head in disapproval. I knew TJ meant no harm by the comment, but it just didn't seem like the kind of thing to joke about. Visions of that poor little boy's mom having to make a decision to donate her precious son's organs sent chills up my spine.

"It is awful. The saddest cases we see are usually motorcycle accidents. And most of the time, they don't make it." I could see the sincerity in TJ's eyes as he shared with me the cause of the little boy's stay in ICU. And I thought to myself how difficult it must be to have TJ's job.

In his world, death was an everyday part of life - seeing patients come and leave - some on their way to recovery and others to their forever home away from this world. It would seem that in order to work in the Nuero-ICU, a person would have to be careless about life - unfazed by the constant flow of lives lost. But, TJ wasn't that way. I could tell. Josh could tell too. TJ was the only nurse Josh would call for

- regardless who was assigned to his shift. If he needed something, he always yelled out, "TJ!"

Josh and I were alone for most of the day. My kids went home with my mother to situate our dogs in a kennel, temporarily, and to pick up some clean clothes. MaeKenna called later in the afternoon and said she had planned to stay with my mom that night, rather than coming back to the hospital.

"That's fine. You need to get some good rest anyway."

"I'm not staying for rest. I've decided to speak at the church tonight and it'll be late by the time service is over," she corrected me.

"You're *talking* at the church?" I asked, wondering if I had misunderstood my daughter.

"Yeah, I'm going to testify about Jesus to the church tonight. Then I'm going to sing a song too." As Maekenna delivered her news to me with a sense of pride and excitement in her voice, I felt concerned.

"Kenna are you sure you're able to do that right now?" I didn't want to discourage her decision, but I was also fully aware of the amount of stress and shock that we were all still under.

"Yeah. God's telling me this is something he wants me to do," my daughter explained. "I can't really say how I know. But I just know he's telling me to do this."

By the night-time, Josh was more wired than ever - still screaming out for water and smoothies. Finally, one of the nurses gave in and brought Josh a cup of ice chips. "He can only have one or two," she warned, as she dropped a small cylinder shaped chip on the tip of his tongue, using a plastic spoon.

Josh was so relieved to get a taste of ice. I was too! And, finally he was able to take a break from begging me to sneak him some water. He rested in naps, much like an infant. Josh slept 2 to 3 hours at a time -

waking up for the routine check-ups where they took his blood pressure and asked him questions.

He usually was able to stay awake in segments of 10 to 20 minutes, until his pain medication kicked back in.

---

**Facebook Post:.**

My brave children are leading a prayer at Woodlands Church right now. MaeKenna volunteered to speak to the youth ministry about what her father is battling through and how God is working in her life, touching this family and healing her dad. I wish Josh and I could be there with the kids to witness my daughter's testimony. But from the distance... I can feel her lifting him up!!

---

"Hi sweetheart, you have a good nap?" I caught myself talking to Josh in a baby voice - like I would use to speak to an infant.

Josh looked at me for a minute and then surveyed his surroundings.

"Baby guess what? Your little girl is testifying about Jesus and singing to the church right now," I informed Josh - excited to tell him the news of MaeKenna's plans.

"Right now?" Josh asked.

"Yep, right now." I confirmed.

"Need to video it." Josh instructed.

"Yeah, Josh Jr. said he would video it and send it to us after she's done," I assured him.

"Who's that?" He asked me, shifting his stare in the direction of the foot of his bed.

"Who's what?" I asked him back - looking around to see who he could possible be referring to.

"Her! Who is she?" Josh asked again. - once more looking at the foot of his bed.

I looked around and saw a nurse standing outside of the glass wall to the side of Josh's hospital room.

"Are you talking about the nurses standing outside?" I inquired, pointing to the wall that was positioned a few feet to the right side of his stare.

"No, not them. I'm talking about her! She's right there!" He seemed frustrated with me and absolute in his claim, as he pointed his right index finger firmly in the direction of the foot of his bed. "She looks kind of like MaeKenna," he explained.

"Are you an angel?" Josh's voice softened as his stare intensified on the empty space.

"You see someone there Josh?" Goosebumps formed on the back of my neck as I watched Josh speaking to an invisible entity.

He ignored me for several moments - despite my desperate list of questioning. His face was soft and peaceful as he stared at the woman that only he could see.

"She's gone now." He announced, turning his eyes back on me.

"What did she say to you?" I asked.

"She said I'm going to be fine." He grabbed my hand and squeezed it tightly.

"What else did she say?"

"I can't tell you." He was so serious and so matter-of-fact about his secret conversation with what I assumed, must have been an angel.

"Why not?" I demanded.

"It's not time. Tell you later." He whispered as he closed his eyes and drifted back to sleep.

I pondered what had happened over the next several hours - Josh's expression on his face and absoluteness in his voice as he encountered an angel at the foot of his bed. He was literally frustrated with me that I couldn't see her - pointing and throwing his hand in the air, as he inspected the subject of his vision. And the strange explanation that he'd now given me twice - first in telling me about his conversation with Jesus, and then with the angel too. Both times he told me that he couldn't tell me what was said to him. Like it was a some sort of divine secret or a message with an appointed date of revealing - he said, "I'll tell you later."

**Facebook Post:**

_____

The only thing more amazing than MaeKenna's testimony tonight.. Is that her father just picked his head up and opened both eyes to watch this video of MaeKenna singing about our Jesus!

_____

Later that night, we cried together in tears of pride as we watched MaeKenna's performance over my cell phone. She sang beautifully with the church band to *Sinking Deep*, by Hillsong United.

I played the testimonial videos one by one, but Josh wasn't able to stay awake long enough to watch them with me. He slept better than usual that night - and even though my bed was a cold, leather hospital chair, I finally slept a few hours too.

**Facebook Post:**

This morning my heart is full. I'm still in amazement with my children - my son Josh Jr., who's spent much of his time the last week reading the bible and praying to God. My daughter, who gave a testimony of God's love at a time that should be humanly impossible. I'm still in ICU with Josh this morning - 11:45 last night marked a full week from that moment when our world turned upside down.

This family is supposed to be shattered in a million pieces, devastated and hopeless. We are supposed to be asking God "Why me?" "Why him?" "Why now?". We are supposed to be swimming in fear and terror and our hearts are supposed to be broken. We are doing none of those things that the Devil has designed - fear is of the enemy.

Jesus said: "With man this is impossible, but with God all things are possible." - *(Mathew 19:26, NIV)*

Watching the videos last night of my daughter telling her story to hundreds of people as she was filled with peace and faithfulness in God's plan for her and for Josh, was simply amazing. HE is working through her to save lives. I hope there were young men and young women who saw her miraculous strength last night and heard her testimony and asked Jesus Christ to enter their hearts as their Lord and Savior.

I know this is only the beginning of her story, Josh's story - our story and God's story.

I will post her full testimony when I receive a link from the church. In the meantime, Josh is leaving ICU today. He's already been cleared, we are only waiting for the room and order to be completed.

70

Here is a photo of Josh's white board in his ICU room. When we checked in here last week they asked me to write my number at the bottom. Below the number I also wrote my confession of faith in what God was going to do. *Thank you Jesus!*

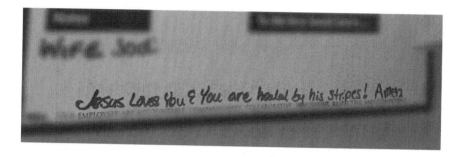

---

After more than a week, it was finally announced that Josh would leave ICU and be transferred to the stroke unit. It was a night of excitement and nervousness too. I thought the worst was behind us and couldn't wait to see Josh leave that place. But less than 30 minutes after the orders were delivered to Josh's room for the transfer, my excitement was abruptly interrupted, as Josh's right eye had produced an irregular reading once again.

Within a matter of seconds, the same exact process started all over as doctors came rushing into his room - making me leave so they could scan his brain and assess what was going on.

I dreaded the news that I knew I just *couldn't* handle again.

*Please Lord, no more surgeries,* I begged under my breath - waiting as patiently as possible from down the hall.

This time, the news was good. While the staff was highly concerned by the fact that Josh's pupil didn't respond to light the way it was supposed to during the exam, the scans showed no change in Josh's brain.

I was allowed to return to the room while they continued to work by Josh's bedside - trading questions and answers between one another.

"Are you sure?" The doctor asked Josh's nurse. Then another man dressed in scrubs stepped forward and responded. "I even double checked after TJ did the exam. The pupil was blown doctor," the man explained.

They looked puzzled as they discussed Josh's eye - shining a small flashlight again and again into his face. And in their confusion, a sense of understanding came over me. It was evident by their discussions that something had mysteriously *changed*. Josh went from having a major issue to having no issue - just like that. The men were questioning one another, wondering how his pupil had miraculously started working correctly again.

I knew how. God had done it.

---

**Facebook Post:**
Last night was a special milestone. After 8 days In ICU, multiple procedures and 2 brain surgeries, Josh is stable and leaving ICU.

I realize we are one step forward with a thousand steps left to go, but I'm confident this journey will lead to a full recovery.

I'm so thankful to our God. It's said He doesn't give us more than we can handle. By faith in Him, our family has handled this tremendous event with strength. God knows we can't lose Josh though.. and that's why he's performing this miracle.

---

# Chapter Four

# *Purpose* In the Pain

## Why God?

Josh's long awaited transfer was bitter sweet. We were finally out of ICU - stable enough to leave the death floor. But there was a strong sense of not belonging in the stroke unit. It looked almost like an elderly home. White haired patients wheeled around the halls, dragging their IV trollies.

Reminders like this were hard to swallow - thinking through the impossible idea of a healthy, handsome, athletic 39-year-old with zero health issues falling victim to a massive brain stroke. Josh didn't even have a primary physician. He just didn't get sick - neither did I. We were like 30-somethings going on 20. We'd always been the young, cool parents at our children's schools. We were both unusually fit and active for our age.

In Josh's spare time he coached little league football and spent countless hours in the gym working out. The kids just loved Josh. He was always playing basketball with a group of boys in our drive-way or working out at the fields with them - throwing footballs and running through drills. Amazingly, Josh could still run the 40 under 5 seconds and dunk a basketball. He was the poster-boy for what most 30-something year old men aspired to look like. *Out of all people, how could this happen to my Josh?* I wondered - several times each day.

Josh's new room was tiny and had a dirty feeling to it. The nurses weren't as attentive on the stroke floor - keeping a larger patient ratio.

Immediately after arriving, a heavy-set man came to Josh's bedside with a young woman following behind him.

"She's an intern in training," he announced to me, signaling to the woman that was shadowing him.

The male nurse went through a series of motions assessing Josh's status and pausing frequently to make notes.

"You want to see something cool?" He asked the young lady - raising his eyebrows in wonder. "Watch this!"

The burly guy raised his palm in the air and then slung his arm forcefully toward Josh's face - like a vicious attack to slap the side of Josh's head. I rose to my feet in shock at the gesture, gasping out loud.

He chuckled as he stopped his hand just before it made impact against the side of Josh's head.

"See that? He doesn't even flinch." His man breasts shook awkwardly in an up and down motion under his scrubs, as he laughed out loud.

"Why doesn't he flinch?" the intern asked.

"He has left neglect. He doesn't even know he owns a left hand or a left leg. His brain ignores the left side of his body. Isn't that cool?"

Hot tears of anger flooded my eyes as I walked around Josh's bed to approach the nurse and his intern - thumbing through my phone.

"It's not cool." I muttered. "And there's nothing comical about what happened to my husband."

The heavyset man's grin diminished as I shoved my cell phone in front of his nose.

"This is what Josh looked like a week ago. If this could happen to him, I hope you understand it could happen to you. What's funny about that?" I asked.

I wasn't trying to come across as confrontational to the nurse and his intern. But I was hurt - hurt for Josh's sake. And in watching the overweight nurse make fun of the aftermath of Josh's stroke that had caused extensive brain damage, I couldn't help but visualize what Josh would say if he were standing in that room healthy.

I knew he wouldn't have to say anything - because that man would've never made fun of the old Josh, standing 6ft. 2, with muscles

74

bulging from underneath his shirt. The old Josh was an image that other men were intimidated by. They feared him and they spoke to him with respect.

"Wow, he's so young." The intern looked over the picture, wearing an uncomfortable expression on her face.

"I wasn't making fun of your husband. This was Josh?" The male nurse seemed to play off the gesture - as if I'd misunderstood his intentions. And I probably did. Maybe he wasn't trying to make fun of Josh. Maybe I was just lost in the process of attempting to swallow the reality that my handsome, tough-guy, husband was now laying helplessly on a floor that was designed for old people - the age bracket that normally suffered the awful thing called stroke.

*— The Picture of Josh I Shared that day:  Josh on the fields
doing what he loved dearly, coaching the kids at Kingwood
Football League —*

A few minutes had passed when a new nurse entered Josh's room pulling a tray of medications behind her.

"What are you giving him?" I inquired - already missing his care staff in ICU, who always explained every move before it was made.

She called off the long list of drugs that she prepared to give Josh.

"He just got all of those before we moved down. It's not time for his medicines." I informed her.

"The computer says I give it - I give it!" She bantered back, taking a fingernail to thump the tube connected to a small needle.

"No! You're going to overdose him! He just got these!" I stood up and placed an arm in front of Josh's IV trolly - guarding my husband against the careless nurse's needle that was now in route to his arm.

She made a loud puffing noise and rolled her eyes at me. Then picked up the phone to dial out. By her aggressive demeanor, I wondered if she was calling security on me.

"Ok. You're right." She concluded after hanging up the phone. "I guess the computer system didn't transfer his updated file to us from ICU." The nurse collected the medicines back to her tray and disappeared around the corner.

It wasn't the last time I'd stop a nurse from making a crucial error in administering drugs to Josh. And the mishaps just added to my determination to stay at his side. Staff members nagged at me constantly to go home and get some sleep.

"You're going to end up going down yourself if you don't rest," The night shift nurse, James warned me repeatedly. But in my mind, I had no choice. Josh was too fragile for me to leave. Plus, every time he woke, he immediately searched the room calling out my name. I couldn't stomach how scared he must feel - waking up in the same nightmare over and over again. The least I could do was be there to hold his hand through it all.

**Facebook Post:**
We are day 3 in stroke unit care, not knowing how fast or slow the next stages will come and go... I hope we will be moved to a recovery room soon. Taking it day by day and loving this man with all my heart.

Thank you God for saving him and for the healing that we are experiencing now. None of this would be possible if Jesus hadn't given his life - taken the worst torture imaginable, and with each stripe He was saving Josh.. Healing Josh. Thank you Jesus for I know this healing is done. God will finish it and this man will fully recover. Amen.

One of the worst nights he'd had yet hit us right as the doctors were considering moving Josh to a regular room. It almost seemed like clock-work. Each time we were about to experience a small victory, (graduating to a lower level of care), the enemy viciously attacked.

His pain was unbearable and Josh had began picking at the stitches on his head - forcing the doctors to tie his only functional arm to the side of his hospital bed.

With his right arm secured, he resorted to using his right leg to cause a commotion - kicking at the bottom bar as hard as he could.

The nurses were frustrated - coming back to his room repeatedly to reposition the tie-downs.

"Josh you stop that kicking!" The heavy-set black woman commanded.

But Josh didn't stop. In fact, he became more violent with every hour that passed. He yelled and screamed, (as loud as he could with his lack of vocal chord control). At one point, he even knocked the bedside table over - creating a huge mess for the nurses to clean.

78

In the midst of his outrage, he glared at me like he hated me. I could feel his anger as he stared me down with black-pupil saturated eyes, watching me closely. He waited for the opportunity to strike me with his leg.

"Why are you trying to kick me Josh?"

"You let them tie me up!" He answered - aggressively trying to free his leg from the strap that connected his foot to the bars under the bed.

This wasn't even Josh. I didn't know who this man was that looked like something out of a horror movie - staring me down with intense fury. And sadly, he was hurting himself with every stroke of his foot against the metal bar. I knew I had to do something.

After fighting with the hospital staff back and forth, I finally convinced them to send the ER doctor on call to check on Josh.

Taking note of my complaints of the drastic change in Josh's personality, the doctor decided to order a scan of his brain.

About a half-hour later, two men showed up to take Josh to the second floor for a brain scan. They allowed me to walk with them as they transported Josh - asking questions about his responsiveness.

**Facebook Post:**

Please help me raise Josh up in prayers right now. Going back to ct-scan.

Josh would have to sit still in order for the scan to work - and he was clearly not in the right mind to listen to instructions. They decided to give him a medicine that would calm him down - and then they wrapped him up so tightly in a cocoon of blankets, Josh was no longer able to move his body at all.

79

He yelled and fought and tossed himself left to right - like a prisoner fighting to break out of chains, until the medicine finally kicked in a calmed him down.

It was a stressful field-trip downstairs, but it also wore Josh out enough to sleep well that night.

---

**Facebook Post:**
After a few tough days, Josh is finally getting some needed sleep. First ct-scan shows swelling and bleeding are still stable. Waiting on results for contrast and artery review.. The doctors said we will know results in the morning.

God is Good and I know these challenges are all part of his plan for healing.

---

I already knew the results of the scan. I have no idea how, but the next morning as the doctor came to deliver the news, I felt God wrapping me in his arms again and revealing *HIS* report even before the doctor could speak.

---

**Facebook Post:.**
As amazing as the neuroscience docs are, it's more amazing how very little is known about the brain.

Latest update: MRI shows Josh has had a second stroke in a small area next to the initial stroke. Meanwhile Ct with contrast shows that Josh's clot in his neck that caused the stroke is almost dissolved. Docs believe as it has dissolved, a small part of the clot moved north into the brain and caused the second stroke.

My interpretation: Although they aren't certain of when the 2nd stroke happened, docs think it may not be a new problem, but may have happened several days ago (I agree). I'm seeing my husband getting better in the last 24 hours. I'm seeing a man regaining his strength and his awareness. I believe the second stroke is in God's agenda for healing because that clot could've moved now, or 5 years from now. HE is making sure that it is done and finished.

Josh prayed out loud this morning... He said..

"Please God, heal me now, make today the day. God please I'm ready to go home to my kids." Of course I broke down in tears hearing his conversation with God, but a comforting feeling warms my heart as I know our Lord will answer Josh's call.

The bad news that seems to keep coming throughout the last 2 weeks has lost its fire over me. No matter what the docs discover or how many times Josh takes a step backward, he's still moving two steps forward and pushing through. There is a bright light at the end of the tunnel that God has prepared for Josh and my eyes are set on that light.

---

The bad news was, Josh had suffered another stroke that night. The good news was that the stroke was caused by a large piece of the clot dislodging itself. That clot would be a lingering fear of death that had remained over Josh's life since the initial stroke took place.

They weren't able to operate on it because the chance of knocking it loose was too high. And if it were knocked loose, it could deliver the final blow to Josh's brain. So they left it there, hoping to control it's movement by giving Josh blood thinners.

81

Well, it had finally came loose, and though it did inflict more damage to another part of Josh's brain, the damage was minimal and Josh was still alive and moving forward.

There seemed to be a pattern to walking in faith. Each time I set my sights on a new destination, whether it was moving down to a lower level of care, or achieving another milestone, a test would follow. Like the night he was to be transferred out of ICU; just an hour before his transfer, Josh's pupil had blown - introducing the possibility of another emergency surgery and deflating the idea of leaving ICU. But I stood in faith and we *did* leave that night. The Lord miraculously corrected the issue within a matter of minutes. Then again, as we were scheduled to leave the stroke unit, Josh was sent for another scan - uncovering a second stroke.

It's almost as if the Lord was saying to me, "Jodi do you have faith I can move him out of the stroke unit tomorrow, *even if* Josh is being sent to emergency scans tonight?"

I had a new understanding of what Paul meant in the Bible when he said, "We walk by faith, not by sight." And I now understood what David saw when he faced that giant standing before him. He saw God - all knowing, all powerful, all capable.... God of the universe.

The Lord was teaching me how to see His promises, instead of the world's report. My eyes looked upon situations that sparked fear. But, my spirit was learning to overcome my eyes - to show me another truth that was more reliable than my physical senses. God was in control and I believed him over the doctors, and over the scans, and even over my own understanding as trouble stared me in the face. *He is faithful. He will do it.* I told myself.

---

**Facebook Post:**

I was tagged in this message from Joel Osteen today...

Joel wrote - "Being a person of faith doesn't exempt you from difficulties. The enemy may hit you with his best shot, but because your house is built on the rock, his best will never be enough. When the storm is over, you will not only come through it, but you'll come out better than you were before...." *(Facebook Page: Joel Osteen Ministries, April 2, 2016)*

I've had visions of the plan all along, intertwined with too many emotions for complete clarity but i do believe this - that our best days are yet to come. God doesn't bring pain and sickness upon us. What happened to Josh was not God's doing. I've never before had such a clear encounter of the enemy - to the extent that I began predicting his moves. Satan doesn't know the future.. The outcome.. This is why he tries so hard. Only God possesses the power to know the future. When we become aligned with God, he shares with us his knowledge and provides us with his strength. He showed me visuals of my family after this passes, visuals of Josh spending time with lil Josh.. Visuals of all of us spending quality family time together.. God doesn't mislead and there is no denying the power of His Word and His faithfulness.. When you BELIEVE and TRUST in Him.

I hope all of my friends and family can truly know God as I'm learning to and the amazing love he has for us - the amazing sacrifice of Jesus Christ and what the unimaginable pain and torture that He endured means for our lives. There is a great promise that is gifted to us. All we must do is surrender to Him.

———

Graduations from ICU to the stroke unit, then down to a so-called regular room in MICU, (minor ICU) presented big expectations that fell short. Each time I would get the news that Josh was being transferred to a different unit, a shimmer of excitement shot through my veins. It was like unspoken hospital language translating the phrase "he's getting better." But as we settled into each transition, I began to realize the only thing that was changing was Josh's level of care.

ICU gifted Josh one nurse appointed only to him. The stroke unit appointed him one nurse - shared between two or three rooms. And in MICU, Josh rarely saw any nurses at all. The few nurses in this unit made rounds every few hours to check on the multitude of patients - leaving Josh's supervision to a monitoring station that watched for changes in his vitals over the many machines hooked to up his body.

What I had hoped would be steps in the right direction with these moves, seemed more like heavier weights placed on my own shoulders. I was more scared to leave Josh, knowing that no one was watching over him. And as I sat at his bedside, hour upon hour, and day after day, I witnessed a type of neglect that made my stomach sour. Even when Josh's machines sounded off alarms of warning, no one came. I would run up the hall to the monitoring station for help, often times receiving no response from the station watchers. They would say things like, "His nurse must be on break. I'll tell her when she gets back." After repeating this process a number of times, I was lucky to be greeted with an eye-roll when I approached the monitoring station.

The inattentiveness from Josh's staff put my nerves on high alert. Obviously, I didn't want Josh to go back to ICU, realizing the prerequisite of patients on that floor requires death to be a looming and probable possibility. But, the difference between ICU nurses and MICU nurses was night and day - not to mention I'd personally interfered on several occasions, as the only reason Josh wasn't overdosed with medications by faulty record keeping. I felt more each day that we were surrounded by people who saw Josh as just another patient - nothing but a number. Like an item stocked on a shelf, Josh was another body in a bracelet, managed by systems, not by love.

Meanwhile, my kids were desperately begging me to come home. They didn't need me - my mother and my step-dad, Jim were taking great care of our children. I think more than anything, they just worried about me and missed me being with them.

"Mom, it's just for one night. You really need to get some sleep," MaeKenna argued over the phone.

"I can't leave him babe."

"Ask Grandma Vivian to stay with him." MaeKenna's idea was a good one, but I hated to bother Josh's mom. Plus, I wasn't the imposing type. I figured if someone wanted to relieve me from watching over Josh for a night, they would offer it without me asking.

"Baby, Grandma Vivian has to go work." I replied, remembering that Vivian had made the comment a few days back that she wished she could see Josh more, but her work schedule was hectic.

Within a few minutes of hanging up the phone with MaeKenna, Josh's mom called my cell phone.

"Hey Jodi, it's Vivian. MaeKenna just called me asked if I could watch Josh so you could come home tonight." I smiled at the thought of my aggressive personality 16-year-old that took matters in her own hands.

"Well, if you're able to I guess it would be nice to see the kids and pick up our mail. Maybe I can pay some bills." I replied.

Around 9 O'clock that night, Vivian arrived at the hospital with her travel bag. I kissed Josh goodbye and headed home for the first time in a month.

## — Remember Your Mother's Dream —

It felt strange making that trip back to our neighborhood without Josh. I hardly even recognized our street after so much time had passed in a 24-7 state of shock, running on adrenaline.

Stepping foot into our living room for the first time since I'd left our home in a hurry that night in March - following behind the paramedics who loaded Josh into an ambulance, was more difficult than I could've ever prepared myself for.

I can't really express where I was mentally, because I was beyond defeated. I tried to act as normal as possible in front of the kids, but then took my first opportunity to run into the spare bedroom, where I cried hysterically with my head in a pillow - hoping the kids couldn't hear me.

I texted my mom and asked her if I could stay with her and then tried to figure out how I would explain to the kids, who were so excited to have me home for the first night in months, that I just couldn't find the strength to be in our home. For me, it was like walking into a crime scene - revisiting the horrid memories of what happened when I saw Josh collapse on our sofa. And opening our bedroom door to see everything was exactly as we'd left it that night, the bedside lamps still lit, i just felt like the air was knocked out of my lungs, like I was about to suffocate. I just had to get out of that house fast - too many things were going through my head - I wondered if Josh would ever step foot back into our home. *Would he ever sleep in his own bed again? Would he ever get to hear the sweet sound of his daughter upstairs in her room practicing music?*

"God, I don't understand. Why would you let this happen?" I sobbed out loud.

It was a real moment of weakness and I remember as I was laying there crying into that pillow, I heard a voice say "I'm not destroying Josh, I'm saving him. Remember your mothers dream."

It was a light-bulb moment that shook me to the core. My mother's dream wasn't a memory I had to search for. Suddenly, I remembered it like it was yesterday - that phone call I received almost a year before Josh's stroke was at the tip of my thoughts as that supernatural voice spoke to my soul.

I was in a rush to get the kids off to school that morning and make my way to work when my mother called me crying.

"Jodi I just had the worst dream ever."

86

I remember thinking to myself, *She's crying about a dream? I don't have time for this.*

"We were all going up one by one."

"Going up where mom?" I interrupted her, fiddling to find my keys that I somehow lost every time I was running late.

"It was the rapture. It was glorious Jodi. As I floated up I saw Jim. Then I saw Tori. Then, my dad - My mother wasn't there for some reason." She paused. "She must have already passed before the rapture. As we were being joined together one by one we celebrated and screamed out Yay! There's Jodi. There's MaeKenna! There's Little Josh! We were so happy to see our family members that were going up with us, gathered together in the sky. Then I looked around and asked you, Jodi! Where's Josh? And then I woke up."

"Mom this is why you're crying? It was just a dream. Josh is saved and he knows who Jesus is." I explained in between yelling at the kids to get downstairs because we were late.

"It wasn't just a dream. It was so real Jodi. I'm worried about Josh. Please just keep him in your prayers."

As I sat up in bed going through that conversation with my mother in my mind, I felt an undesirable sense of peace come over me. It was the Lord's voice that had spoken into me, showing me His love - which seems impossible because everything was so broken. *How can that be His love?* Because he knows things we don't. Yes, it's His love. I've read many stories in the Bible about refinement - about judgement starting with the church. And as I pondered the meaning of "the church" those who are the body of Christ, (it's not a physical building), I embraced the beautiful moment upon me - hearing the Lord speak to me with revelation about his perfect plan, and feeling his peace as he calmed me down and gave me understanding about a process that was for our good.

The greatest gifts are coming to the vessels that have nothing of themselves in them, and everything of Jesus. All must be purged and that process hurts - it can sting so badly we see no immediate hope in a future that's good - but it's the process of something beautiful in the making.

It's hard to rejoice in our trials but there's a reason for the things we go through, for the qualifying - buying Gold of Jesus "tried by the fire". There's a reason the apostles said to rejoice through our fiery trials. This night and that message about my mothers dream would be a stone that I would carry throughout our journey. The Lord knew I needed a message - he knew I needed understanding. And though this wouldn't be the last time that I would fall apart overcome by fear and hopelessness, I had part of my "why?". God said, he's saving Josh and I believe him.

*Consider it pure joy, my brothers and sisters, whenever you face trials of many kinds, because you know that the testing of your faith produces perseverance. Let perseverance finish its work so that you may be mature and complete, not lacking anything. - (James 1:2, NIV)*

———————

**Facebook Post:**
I came home tonight to see my kids and get some needed rest. Vivian is staying at the hospital with Josh and they moved him to a recovery room tonight. It's great to have him sleeping peacefully outside of ICU and the stroke unit. My baby has had a tough 2 weeks. He's been so strong and I am forever grateful for the fight that he's made and continues to make for me and the kids.

I bought this little wood thing right before his stroke.. Found this old photo from the night we got engaged and placed them next to one another on our bedroom dresser. It's emotional seeing our bedroom.. But this... Well, it reminds me of where we're going. God gave me Josh for a reason. I was lost when I met him... He was a little lost too. We were just kids back then and neither of us had a clue about life.. But together we figured it out. We spent most of our years just the two of us trying to raise two kids in parts of the country where we knew no one. We didn't need anyone though. He was my rock and I was his.

Sixteen years later, I love him more than ever and I'm so thankful to God for blessing my life with this man. I will forever be grateful to Jesus for the miracle he's performing in our lives right now. Thank you God for your mercy and your faithfulness. Thank you for not taking him with you and for knowing how much we still need him here. It may not happen overnight but I know God will finish this miracle and heal Josh completely!

Josh - so thankful God gave me You...

---

*— The Picture I took of our bedroom dresser. This is how I'd left it that night Josh suffered the stroke in our home - purchasing the "God gave me you" sign, just hours before he went down.. —*

# — *I Keep Bleeding Love* —

On Saturday night, my daughter invited me to attend the Spring Show with her at the high school. It was a night of performances, (ballet kind of performances) put on by the AHS dance team.

Walking in, we saw familiar faces - many of the moms stared at me like they'd seen a ghost. A few of them came up to ask about Josh and give me hugs. It was nice to get out and it was also nice to do my hair and wear make-up for a change.

The show was beautiful. After the group performances, some of the dancers took turns doing solo dances. One of the seniors danced to the song "bleeding love." As the familiar melody began to play over the theater loud speakers, I felt like something was closing my eyes shut. The whole point of the show was to watch the dance, but I couldn't look up - and then I stopped trying when I felt that great sense of peace that I'd felt the night before in our spare bedroom come over me once more.

As the lyrics penetrated my mind like a drug making its journey through my veins, I saw HIM...

*You cut me open and I... Keep bleeding... Keep, keep bleeding love.. I keep bleeding love...*

I can't explain how I know that it was Jesus - I just knew. With my eyes closed tightly, I saw a set of eyes staring into my soul - so deeply - so full of love and compassion that I felt paralyzed in his perfect peace. His eyes were made of colors I'd never seen - swirling and churning like a raging fire. And in the blackness that surrounded his fiery, majestic eyes I saw His blood pouring out over me like a waterfall of Grace.

As the song repeated the words that were captivating my heart in the most intimate and beautiful moment I'd ever known, *"I keep bleeding.. I keep..keep bleeding love.."* I sat there in a pool of my own tears, forgetting all of my surroundings. I didn't worry that someone may see me crying. I didn't care that I was surrounded by hundreds of parents and teenagers from our community. There was no embarrassment, or fear - there wasn't even a me in that moment. There was just Jesus and his blood of salvation - the fire of his loving eyes and his perfect peace pouring out upon me.

*Revelation 19:12 - And his eyes were as a flame of fire, and on his head were many crowns; and he had a name written, that no one has known, but he himself.*

## — *Everyone's Under Attack* —

Sunday morning I woke up early to pack a bag and head back to the hospital. Feeling refreshed, rested and in a state of absolute peace after the amazing encounters with God, I was excited to get back to Josh's bedside and help him adjust to his new regular room. Today was the big day that we would celebrate another milestone on our journey - graduation from the stroke unit.

I was just getting in the car when I got the call from my mom. She said that my Granny had been transferred from the nursing home to an emergency room in Clear Lake and the doctors believe she had suffered a stroke. The news was surreal - how could this happen to two people in my life within a matter of weeks apart? No one I knew had ever had a stroke. Now, Josh and my Granny were in this tragic boat together?

I called Vivian and asked her if she could stay with Josh a few more hours so that I could go visit my Granny in the ER. Then drove as fast as I could to reach my family in the waiting room of the small hospital.

My Granny wasn't attentive and I immediately recognized the familiar equipment hooked up to her head - she was on life support. My Papa explained that the doctors had reported my Granny was currently in a coma, as I held her hand and tried to speak with her.

"Let's pray over her," I suggested. Holding hands with my papa and my mom over Granny's bed, I prayed out loud, speaking the words of Isaiah 53:5 - "By the stripes of Jesus, you are healed!"

When I concluded my long and heartfelt prayer, I was at peace - an inner-knowing came over me, like an absolute revelation that she was going to be fine. This was a place I had become accustomed to - a place of courage, understanding that my Lord and Savior heard my prayers. He listened and he cared.

"She's going to be ok, Papa." I whispered as I hugged him tightly and picked up a tear from his cheek with my finger.

He nodded in agreement but wore a look of worry in his eyes.

"No, I mean it Papa. I feel the Lord's peace on this and he's telling me that Granny is going to make it through this."

With confidence in my Granny's stability, I hugged everyone again and then departed for the med center to relieve Vivian and return to Josh.

When I arrived at Josh's new floor, a nurse directed me to Josh's room - walking with me to show me the way. Josh was the center of attention as my daughter had rode with Jason, his brother, and his girlfriend, Jess. He had a room full of people surrounding him and talking with him.

"Hi baby!" I announced myself from the doorway. As Josh spoke back to me, telling me about his new room, something strange happened - the corners of the room started closing in on me. My peripheral vision decreased and blankets of blackness narrowed my sight.

I took a step back, then everything went black.

The next thing I knew, I was in a wheelchair directed by the nurse that had shown me to Josh's room.

"Where are we going?" I asked her - the long hallway we traveled was spinning in circles around me.

"I'm taking you to the ER. How are you feeling?" She asked, half-way out of breath as she hurried to push me.

"My hands are numb and I can't feel my legs. I'm spinning." I admitted - confused by the symptoms that I was witnessing in my body.

Kenna had come along with us and I was relieved to see her at my side, feeding information to the check-in desk on the ER floor.

"I called your mom." She told me, as she stroked a lock of hair from my face.

Within a matter of minutes I was in a hospital bed, hooked up to an IV. My mother and Jim joined us at some point and relieved MaeKenna to return upstairs with her dad.

"Don't tell him Kenna. It could make his blood pressure spike." I instructed my daughter as she kissed me on the cheek *goodbye*.

The ER doctors assessed me for stroke and then concluded that I was on the verge of having a nervous breakdown.

"Your body is trying to shut down. You've been through a lot and the anxiety and stress is going to take you down if you don't find a way to rest."

Feeling better, I shrugged off the doctor's recommendation to keep me overnight and signed release papers so I could get back upstairs to Josh.

That night, even more strange news would come. In a 12-hour period, my granny had suffered a stroke and I had passed out with a severe panic attack. Later I would get a call from my daughter - crying because of intense stomach pain. "I can't get even get up mom. It hurts so bad!" Then a few minutes after that, my mother reported that she

94

missed being plowed by a truck driving over 80 going down the wrong way of Highway 59.

---

**Facebook Post:**

Request - please help!! I ask all of my friends, family, even complete strangers to raise my family up in your prayers tonight. We have seen lives change, love conquer and God rising Josh up into a miracle. We have also seen consistent attacks from Satan coming from many directions... My grandma is now in ICU. I was admitted to the ER this afternoon. My mother barely escaped a bad car accident on the way home from the hospital and then my daughter had an attack of stomach illness hit her this evening.

The enemy is attacking but he is losing over and over again. In agreement, let's all put the enemy away for good! Please pray with me.....

In this video Maekenna sang to Josh tonight as all of our hearts were heavy with love, gratitude, hope and faith in what the Lord has done so far and continues to do for our family. We are all fighting for Josh and we will not lose because Jesus has our backs!

---

*[Note]: Video of Kenna singing to her dad is archived in media section of www.79ministry.com.*

      The attacks kept coming but I kept believing. To know that you're in a war is to understand the process of battle. And for me, the war was spiritual. The enemy wasn't allowed to kill any of us - but he was allowed to test our faith - bringing one incident after the next into my sight. He was desperately grasping to steal the confidence that I'd gained in my Lord.  But no matter how hard he tried, he was going to lose.

*For we wrestle not against flesh and blood, but against principalities, against powers, against the rulers of the darkness of this world, against spiritual wickedness in high places. - (Ephesians 6:12)*

## Blog Entry: *Understanding Why*

My son called me tonight and we talked for a long while.  He opened up to me about some things that were difficult for him lately - feelings, worries...  Then he said, he didn't understand why this happened to his Dad, because his Dad is a great person.

I think this is an important question because it's the one that most people who have suffered a traumatic event or a loss of a loved one is tempted to ask. We ask, "why me?" or "why him?"... I've seen this approach used widely by non-believers and without doubt I believe this is one of Satan's favorite tricks to slide into our thoughts.  He wants us to question God and he tells us that rational thinking would suggest that if God loves his children, he would protect them from bad things happening. Satan wants us to feel betrayed by God and even question his existence in wake of tragedies.

Was Jesus Christ a good person?  If God would send his only son here to be tortured and sacrificed on the cross, what gives us the idea that life as a child of God is supposed to be without trials?

I explained it to my son by talking football.  I said, Josh.. If you're playing against a team that has this crazy good, superstar player who scores all of their points for them.  Which player will your team go after the hardest?  Of course, he said, "We would all focus on their best kid." So, which people do you think Satan is focused on attacking?

Truth is, some events that took place in our family over the last year have made us shift focus a bit. I was probably the most impacted from a standpoint of making it a point to strengthen my faith and my focus on God. But we were still far away from where I believe we're going with our relationships with Jesus. I believe Satan took notice of the blessings that were charted in our future. I believe that Satan saw us as a threat. I have other thoughts as it relates to what could be in store for Josh and his personal relationship with God - and what he may be called to do when he's fully recovered. But just focusing on this one subject as it relates to the topic of discussion with my son, I want to reiterate that God doesn't do bad things to us.
God didn't give Josh this stroke. God did however answer his call and our call - he saved Josh's life and he continues to work on Josh - he is perfecting a miracle of healing in Josh.

We know in everything we do in life that nothing worth having comes easy. Walking in God's light is the ultimate achievement not only to be able to fulfill our purpose here but to have eternal life as a believer of Jesus Christ who died for us. Again, no one said it will be easy. Satan attacks those who he sees as the biggest threats to his purpose - he seeks to destroy our relationship with God.

*— Photo of Josh training our son, Josh Jr. for football —*

# *Afterthoughts...*

When tragedy struck our lives, unexpectedly, it was hard to imagine that something so awful could somehow be part of God's plan.

I remember a repetitive theme placed before me as many of our Christian friends attempted to answer the question "why" by reciting this scripture to me, "Satan comes to kill, steal and destroy."

Perhaps, when we're outside, looking in - watching people in the midst of their suffering, as Christians we feel it's our duty to defend God. We conclude that a good God would never bring heartache and suffering into our lives. And therefore, it's the enemy's fault.

Looking back on the experience I had in our spare bedroom that night when God spoke to me about what HE was doing, (saving Josh), it's clear to me that his hand was present even in our suffering - not as a God that was battling the enemy, trying to help us out. God is God. God doesn't try to do anything. God's plans aren't always comfortable but they're perfect - working for our good, even when we can't see it yet.

In the life of Job, the Bible tells a story of a man that God loved very much. But as Job went through horrific loss and unthinkable trials, he struggled to understand why. Even his friends had the opinion that Job had done something bad to deserve the cards he'd been dealt - implying that God's favor had left Job or that he was perhaps being punished by God. And while Satan was inflicting pain upon Job, he could do nothing outside of God's approval. The enemy was required to obey God as he tortured Job.

In the end, after Job had endured his season of great suffering, God blessed Job's life - returning all he had lost 10-fold. Sometimes great loss doesn't offer reward on this side of glory. But through the cross that Christ defeated, we can be assured that all things work for the good of those who love the Lord, and when he finishes our race here, life everlasting will reveal beauty that we can't even comprehend.

God didn't give Josh a stroke. But he did allow it to happen. And I believe he will reveal great purpose and great Glory even through the ashes - he paints beauty.

# Chapter Five

# *Choose* Life

## He Makes My Paths Straight

Each afternoon the physical therapy guys would stop by Josh's room with the same routine. The short, older gentleman would clap his hands together and say, "Josh! Are you ready Josh?" Even though these brief visits were repetitive, I couldn't help but get my hopes up when I saw the PT guys enter his room. I would pray to myself, "Let today be the day Lord." As the tiny man grunted and strained to try and get Josh's limp body into an upright position, I visualized the miracle that I so longed for. I could almost see Josh, snapping into the powerful frame of a man that I had always known him to be and jumping out of the bed. I would scream out, "Thank you God! It's a miracle! Josh is healed!" And as silly as my imagination may have seemed to anyone other than me, something deep inside my soul believed that one of these days that vision would become a reality. I thought back upon the image that captivated my thoughts on that dreadful night of Josh's last surgery. The doctors had quickly and unemotionally prepared me for the worst before wheeling Josh away in a heated hurry to open up his brain, yet again. God showed me Josh healed as I laid there curled up in the fetal position on the empty floor of Josh's ICU room. Even if no one other than me could believe in what I saw, I knew it to be truth. It was a tender touch of hope delivered to to me as a gift from Heaven, and I will never quit expecting that vision to come to life before my eyes.

"I heard that you're trying to get Josh into TIRR," the shorter man inquired through his broken English accent. "Yes, I'm visiting the facility later today," I nodded.

He flicked his index finger and signaled for me to join him as he walked backward to the corner of Josh's room."You didn't hear this from me. But he has to go to TIRR." The PT's expression was serious and frank.

"But the doctors keep telling me that it's too risky to move him out of here." I confessed - shifting through the consistent conversations that had taken place recently. Josh's team of doctors had approached me at least half a dozen times to insist that Josh was too sick to leave their care. They recommended that I leave him in the hospital with limited therapy, warning that if Josh needed another emergency surgery there may not be enough time to transfer him back by ambulance.

"We can't give him the therapy he needs here. He needs intense rehab and if he were my brother or my son, I would send him to TIRR."

The PT's honesty was evident and although he didn't know it, he was giving me the answer that I'd prayed effortless for. I was terrified by the doctors' warnings. But I was more terrified at looking Josh in the eyes one day and admitting that I didn't make the right decisions for him. To make matters even more difficult, I'd somehow found myself in an unspoken battle with Josh's mother over this move.

Vivian didn't approach me directly to discuss Josh's next move - the big decision to send him to TIRR or leave him in the hospital. But she did make remarks in my direction during her last few visits to the hospital. Surrounded by Josh's other family members, she made comments to indirectly question my thoughts relating to Josh's care.

"All I know is, that the doctor told me that he is not stable enough to leave here." She explained to Josh's dad as the two hovered over his bedside.

I couldn't combat the highly skilled team of physicians that were treating Josh with anything based on experience. They knew much more than I did about stroke and about the risks involved with Josh's prognosis. But inside of me, something tugged at me - pushing me into the direction of leaving that place.

Not many people can understand *gut feelings* - that intuition from something bigger and greater than us. They're difficult to explain

101

and hold no proof. In the midst of this important transition, I felt very alone - like an outsider, made the target in an invisible war - I could feel the tension when Josh's family held conversations about the next steps for Josh.

And adding to the stress, Josh was horrified by the idea of staying in that hospital. "I can't stay here another day! I feel like I'm in prison!" He would yell out, disrupting the family discussions that took place in his hospital room. Josh wanted to get back to life. He wanted to walk out of that hospital and never look back. Josh wanted to live again - not stay confined to a set of machines surrounded by doctors and nurses.

------

**Facebook Post:**

Feeling the winds of change today. Josh and I talked a lot last night. He said he has lots to tell me when we get out of here.. His encounters are tremendous, "life changing" as he described it. He told me he wants to buy me a new ring and renew our vowels. He said he has so many big plans.. I can hardly wait to see what Jesus is working on with Josh.

At 2 pm the therapy team came around. They woke him up and said "what do you want to do today Josh?". His answer, "walk out of here."..

A few minutes later he was standing up with the their support. He lifted his head to look at me and then took two steps forward. He stood on his feet another two minutes to their countdown and I'm so proud of his strength and his will power. He will be walking soon on his own. I see the fire in his eyes and the determination to fulfill God's plan. Thank you Jesus, your miracle continues to fill my heart with faith... love and appreciation.

------

It was an awful feeling to be torn between what I felt was right for Josh in my heart and satisfying Josh's family. This was especially difficult as the doctors agreed with Vivian and Josh's care staff aggressively shared opinions of the risks involved with moving Josh out of the hospital.

Visiting TIRR wasn't what I'd expected. The facility was literally walking distance from the hospital where Josh was in care. I wondered why the doctors made such a big deal about *transfer time in case of an emergency.* Quite honestly, the concern seemed almost silly. If something did happen to Josh, it wouldn't take more than a few minutes to get him back to the ICU unit. It was strange that the distance was their main point of argument when the distance seemed to be nothing.

I walked in excited to see this highly rated rehabilitation center. But I ended up passing out. I guess I never really thought about what the move meant. Or maybe I expected this place to be different from the last - TIRR just looked like another hospital. It was another building full of long hallways, doctors coats, nurses and fluorescent lights. It wasn't home. After spending more than a month living inside four collapsing walls, I was eager for something new in Josh's journey. Yes, I wanted him to get better, but I wanted him to come home. Realizing we were headed to yet another care unit in this long, drawn out nightmare that didn't' seem to have an end in sight, I was overwhelmed with grief and anxiety.

The facility wasn't impressive, making the decision more difficult. And again, if I moved him, I would be going against not only the advice of Josh's doctors, but also his mother. On the other hand, the PT attending to Josh inside the hospital had said "if it were my son, I'd send him to TIRR." *What do I do?*

In a haze, I walked to my car slowly. I was in a rush to get back to Josh as usual, with that lingering urgency that something might go wrong while I was away. But I couldn't go back without an answer. I sat in the drivers seat of my Yukon and rested my tearful face on the steering wheel. Then I asked myself, *"If Josh were in his right mind and making this decision. What would he choose?"*

I heard a voice inside of me, clear as day whisper.....

*"He'd choose life."*

I knew without a doubt at that moment that I was moving Josh to TIRR. If I believed that God was healing him, how could I make decisions for Josh based on fear - which is the opposite of faith. It was settled. We were transferring to TIRR.

The morning of transfer, one of the stroke doctors stopped in to deliver instructions and have me sign the electronic release for Josh's move out of the hospital.

"Oh, wait a second. He's still on a feeding tube." She sifted through a stack of papers - looking up at Josh again with confusion on her face.

"He can't transfer out until he's eating on his own."

This was awful news. TIRR wasn't just a *whenever he's ready* kind of option. I learned during my visit at the rehab facility that Josh's release was perfect timing because a room, (one room) was coming available on the brain injury floor. Typically, there was a waiting list to get into TIRR.

"Doctor, please. We can't lose this room. He's eating pudding and they've been counting his calories."

Josh had just been cleared to start taking in liquids and soft foods by mouth a few days ago, after he barely passed the water swallow test.

"I'll have to speak to the nutritionist." She responded, then disappeared around the corner, still writing notes in her booklet.

Within the hour, his internists arrived with great news. She had signed off on the approval for Josh to have the feeding tube removed.

**Facebook Post:**

He was NOT happy about them making him wear a helmet for the transport but he is officially OUT of acute care!!! Josh's new temporary home is TIRR.. Rated the top rehabilitation facility in the nation. A lot of his recovery will come as the swelling in his brain still has a long way to go . But the other part of the journey starts now. This is where Josh shows the world how tough he really is.. As he would say to his kids he's coached "it's time to go to work!"... Continuing to thank God that we are going forward instead of backward and for keeping us all strong through this long, difficult process. Please keep your prayers coming. God's miracle is going to be perfected.

That evening Josh was transferred to TIRR by ambulance. And that message that I had received sitting in my truck, would be confirmed sooner than I even expected!

Immediately upon his arrival he began receiving visitors. His new care team was composed of a speech therapist, an occupational therapist and a physical therapist. All were very nice and cheerful but his physical therapist, which visited Josh last, was a messenger. Kyle looked a lot like Josh had before the stroke. He was not as tall as Josh, but young and very fit, with muscles bulging under the sleeves of his shirt. Right away they clicked. Something I hadn't seen sparkled new in Josh's eyes as Kyle spoke to him. Josh seemed almost excited as he assured Kyle, "I'm ready to get going and get better so I can walk out of here."

After the assessment, Kyle pulled me outside to go over schedules and his plan for Josh in the coming days. I tried to pay attention to the information, but my mind was absent - thinking about the change I'd just noticed in Josh. That was the most alert I'd seen him since the stroke.

"Kyle, I'm so excited," I beamed. "Josh told you he's ready to walk out of here." Kyle nodded and smiled, probably thinking I was spaced out with the strange obsession over Josh's words.

"No you don't understand." I moved in closer to Kyle so I could whisper. "Josh tells me daily that he fears he's about to die. This is the first time I've heard him talk about getting better."

For a moment I thought Kyle's eyes were churning up tears as he studied my face.

"When a guy Josh's age goes through something like this, it's hard for us to understand that he's in shock and he does think he's dying. This has been very scary for him and he knows people who are dying need a hospital. People who are living leave that hospital," Kyle explained.

Our new journey was an emotional roller coaster of 5-day a week therapy with high expectations. Each day I told myself - *This is the day Josh will walk again.* But each day ended with little progress to note in my journal.

Josh spent the first week in PT learning how to hold his head up on his own for more than 5 seconds. Prior to moving to TIRR, he'd been in a hospital bed 24/7. Now that he was required to dress in regular clothes, travel by wheelchair, and transfer to a matt for exercises, everything he couldn't do was placed on display.

It was hard for me to watch - Josh struggling just to lift his chin off of his chest. It took two bodies, placed to his front and back just to keep him from falling over on the matt.

Speech therapy sessions were even worse.

"Josh, I'm going to start my stop watch. When I say GO, I want you to name as many animals as you can within a minute, OK?" His therapist was a sweet, young girl. She was nice but I could tell that her job was *just a job* to her. I'd tried to talk about Josh's life before his stroke with all of his therapists. They pretended to care, but only Kyle truly seemed to.

"Dog…….. Cat………………………………………

….Rabbit…………."

"Ok, time is up." In an entire minute. Josh could only name three animals. The severity of his brain damage was hard to look past in my hopes that he would ever be back to normal again.

My favorite part of our day had become prayer and devotional messages. After Josh had his breakfast each morning, I'd get out my laptop and read our *message for the day*. Then I'd talk with Josh about what I felt the scripture and messages meant for us. And I'd end our talk grabbing Josh's hands in mine and praying with him to our Father in Heaven.

In the evenings we would save our prayer sessions for after Josh ate dinner. Then we would watch TV together - usually switching between presidential election coverage and christian networks.

Sometimes, we would lay there and talk to Rex - Josh's roommate that laid in the bed next to him, separated only by a curtain. Rex was good for Josh, even though it took awhile for Josh to respond to him. Rex talked a lot and he had a humorous personality. Usually he'd ask Josh questions about our family and our kids. I would end up answering the questions because Josh wasn't able to hold a conversation very well. Rex would cut jokes about the nurses and scream out, "I just saw a polar bear walk by, could you make it any colder in this room!" Josh laughed. He enjoyed Rex's company. I enjoyed him too.

**Facebook Post:**

I just want to say I love you all and I'm so thankful for your prayers. The power of prayer is undeniable. I'm not ready to share the details of this journey and may not be for some time, especially as we have a long way to go. But I want everyone to know without a doubt God is real. Josh will be testifying one day of his amazing encounters. I have my own as well. Faith over fact is not an illusion. I've heard the powerful voice speaking over the doctors and HE has been right. He is the truth. If you don't have Jesus Christ in your heart... If you are looking to him everyday for guidance - listening to him for understanding of the purpose he has for you here on Earth.. A day may come when the enemy accesses your weakness. Life is fragile and it can be changed or taken from you at any moment. Be ready and be with Christ.

---

Arriving at TIRR was like making a huge step in the direction of choosing life, instead of fear. But, as Josh and I struggled to find normalcy in our new temporary home - almost pretending at times that the storm was over, the attacks from the enemy kept coming our way. Almost nightly, we were reminded of the looming possibility of complications over Josh's brain, as the irregular and unpredictable swelling continued to be an issue. I hated watching him moan and complain of the migraine headaches - begging for more pain medicine.

But for me, I chose to view those terrifying moments like tiny bumps in the road - small detours on the path to healing that I believed God had in store for us.

I prayed and I believed in prayer. In my heart of hearts I knew deep down that in releasing the word of God in faith, I had power over those attacks. My collection of weapons had expanded - and with each day I searched out the good. I shared stories, testimonies and scriptures with Josh - discussing with my husband the good news of hope - of our savior Jesus Christ, and refusing to give an ear to the lies of the enemy.

---

**Facebook Post:**
Last night I shared a video with Josh that was posted on my Facebook page about a young man who drowned. He was only 19. His parents were told to hurry and catch a plane to say goodbye, with a warning that he may not make it until their arrival, and even if he did make it, he would be brain dead.

108

Satan was lying to that family. The young man made a full recovery - this video brought Josh and I both to tears... Then something amazing happened.

You see last night wasn't a good night. Josh's swelling worsened and he said he was in the worst pain since the initial attack. He had told me he was worried. Not only that, the doctor made mention of it on his nightly rounds and said they needed to watch him closely and may need to run a ct-scan.

Josh told me he could feel the pressure building behind his eye and after 3 PRN doses of pain medicine he was still in severe pain... So with all that in mind.. After we watched the video together, I told Josh I was going to let him be, so he could try to rest, hoping the pain meds would start to work.

A few minutes later he called out to me and asked me to hold his hand. He started to pray out loud, he asked God to heal him, to take his pain away and reminded God that he wants to get home because his children need him. He prayed in Jesus name and then closed his eyes and went to sleep.

Josh has always been a Christian. He tells me he prays.. But laying there thinking about it.. I realized I'd never actually heard him pray out loud with me. In ICU he'd said a few short lines repeating my prayers.. But not like this.. Not *HIS* idea.. Not him taking the initiative to ask me to join him in prayer.

He woke up feeling much better and the swelling had gone back down. Thank you Jesus! Thank you to Keith also for sending the story of your son's near-deaths experience. I know it was inspirational to Josh and gave him faith to reach out to God last night in the midst of his swelling attack.

---

109

# Chapter Six

# *Purple* Stones

## His Paintbrush is Everywhere

For my 37th birthday, Vivian and my daughter planned to give me a break away from the hospital life. On Friday night, Josh's mom arrived at TIRR with the kids. They spent about an hour talking with their dad - taking turns laying next to him in the hospital bed. Then, Vivian announced that she was going to stay with Josh until Sunday, so that I could do something fun with the kids Saturday, in celebration of my birthday.

I could tell MaeKenna was excited - she'd planned that we would get our toes done and then see a movie and go out for a nice dinner. I appreciated her thoughtfulness. She bought me a new bible and had pieced together a frame that read "I Love Mom". Inside of the picture frame was a photo of Josh, MaeKenna and I from several years back, taken at dinner.

Also in the birthday bag, attached to a set of balloons, she gave me a small prayer box, filled with scriptures of hope. It was an emotional moment when she gave me these gifts - a time of reflection on how much things had changed and how much we had grown closer as a family.

My daughter was after my own heart, as a kindred spirit that not only knew my pain and my struggles, but she knew my hearts desires too. I loved the word of God - it had become my blanket of comfort and my best friend that I took with me everywhere I went. The new bible from MaeKenna was beautifully bounded in a purple colored leather. I didn't think much about the color at the time. I just knew that I cherished that great gift, dearly.

*— My birthday gift from my daughter: The Purple Bible —*

I had a great day with MaeKenna and really enjoyed the time spent that evening with both my kids, Kenna and Josh Jr. Life almost seemed normal - they argued over who was taller and took turns picking on one another, as we all laughed together.

But the empty chair at our table for four, as we ate at the popular steakhouse, was a looming reminder of a celebration far from joyous. It was the first time in over 20 years that I'd celebrated a birthday without Josh. The bitterness of loss was offset with hope in a future that would soon re-unite us together again. I laughed a lot and I cried a lot. It was a birthday dinner I would never forget.

The next morning I woke to the sound of my cell phone notifying me of a new text message. It was Josh!

**Facebook Post:**
He may be wounded..but he was the first to call me this morning and tell me Happy Birthday.. Running some errands with the kids this morning, then back to TIRR.. Can't wait to see Josh today!

When we arrived at the hospital, Josh's face immediately lit up with excitement. He reached out his right arm to give me a big hug from his hospital bed. "Happy birthday! I love you so much," he whispered. I could hear the moisture of tears forming in his voice.

He signaled at the hospital tray standing next to his bed, where a card and a small gift box was positioned next to his water bottle.

I could tell by the strange handwriting that his mother had written the card for him. But the words were all his. Josh talked about how blessed he was to have me as his wife. Then he talked about how much he looked forward to our future together - saying that on this day next year, he would plan the biggest birthday celebration ever for me. In closing, he introduced the gift that was in the small box. He said "This gift is a renewal of my vows to you. I will love you and cherish you until the day I die."

With tears flowing down my cheeks, I opened the little box and popped open the lid to reveal a beautiful purple stone ring.

*— My purple stone ring pictured next to the wedding ring Josh had given me when he proposed 18 years ago —*

When I was a little girl I chose the color purple to dress my horse up, in a purple blanket and purple bridle. As I grew older, I didn't really have a favorite color - certainly not one that I'd ever discussed with Josh or the kids.

But as I was learning with so many parts of our journey, the purple stone had great significance and meaning to my life now. I thought about the coincidence of the purple bible that Kenna had gifted me. *Was there such thing as coincidence?*

In the book of Mark, we learn that the soldiers clothed Jesus in a purple robe before they beat him and took him to the cross to be crucified. It is thought by many, that the color purple symbolizes royalty, and may have been used as a form of mockery as they shunned Jesus and laughed, calling him the King.

But as people who looked upon Jesus wearing that purple robe on the way to his death, saw his life ending in torture, suffering and demise, Jesus saw beyond the cross that he carried. He saw the glory that was soon to be His, by the promises of his Father in Heaven.

Maybe in some way, this was significant to my own path that stood before me - unknown and full of great challenges. Maybe, I was being prepared to carry my cross - being taught to look beyond my circumstances to see a destination that was promised in the sacrifice of Jesus.

My purple stone was symbolic of purpose in all the moments of this thing called life - an understanding in places deep inside of me, but an idea that I couldn't fully understand, just yet.

---

**Facebook Post:**

Josh had his mom write for him to fill out my birthday card and he asked her to buy me a ring. It's a beautiful purple stone ring from the gift shop of TIRR. I love it! So his card says April 17, 2017 he wants to hold the biggest celebration ever and he wants to renew our wedding vows. I'm excited about what life has in store for us and what we will be talking about this time next year.

––––––––––

Perhaps the celebration, or lack-of between Josh and I on my birthday was a milestone of searching for understanding inside of Josh too. That night was a big change from the single-sentence discussions we normally had together. He wanted to talk, really talk about what had happened. And sadly, it was eye-opening for me too, in realizing how little he actually knew about his circumstances.

––––––––––

## Blog Entry - *Waking up to Missing Pieces*

Tonight felt different. There was a familiarity in the air when I was talking to Josh - a sense of recognition. Josh wanted to communicate beyond me asking questions and him providing one-line answers. His mind was wandering to places it hadn't before attempted to go since the stroke.

We talked about his head injury and he told me that he worried it was hard for the kids to see him like this. I asked, "because of the skull indention?" He shook his head to say yes. I told Josh that the kids were OK with his appearance because they fully understood what had happened and what would be done going forward.

We talked about how the doctors would soon replace the skull piece and I explained that the kids had been educated on the entire process. "It's not hard for them to see you Josh, it's hard for them to be away from you." I assured him.

That exchange prompted the conversation that I had been anticipating for some time. Josh asked me to tell him what

116

happened that night. It was hard and I didn't get through many details before tears found my eyes.

I was honest with him. I don't think I should downplay the severity of what we went through because he needs to know the truth - that my life will never be the same. He needs to know that what I saw will forever weigh on my mind, threatening the lifeblood of everything that matters to me. You see, I love my family more than anything. But that all starts with Josh.

I see that fifteen year old girl that I used to be - she was lost and closed off to the world. Only he could rescue me from myself and only I could change him too. He was my whole life and I was his. Our kids aren't here because we planned the perfect family and thought through a future that made sense. There was nothing "Brady Bunch" about anything Josh and I did. We struggled and we made lots of mistakes, but through everything we got wrong, there was one thing that we never had to question - one thing that we always got right.. *We loved each other unconditionally.*

I've loved him from the very first moment I saw him. It was like a light-bulb came on inside of me and I knew that he was going to be a big part of my life.

So, yeah, when I saw my soulmate, my best friend, go away to another place right before my eyes, something inside of me died. I felt like I was caught in a cave under the sea, suffocating, yet unsure if I wanted to find my way back to the surface - unsure if I wanted to catch my breath, because breathing in a world that didn't include Josh wasn't a world that I could live in.

The terror that came over me could never be described by words. And, the memory of what I saw and what I felt can never be forgotten.

Josh said that he remembered the severity of the pain in his head before the stroke. He even said he remembered the ambulance drivers, "I can see their faces," he whispered. But he knew nothing else of the evening.

"You were talking about football, and then you just laid down on your side." I explained. Josh said that he remembered he was sitting on the couch. He was right. Josh was curled up over the large arm of the ottoman side of our sectional in the living room. One minute he was carrying on with Jim about the NFL, and then in the next, his body collapsed to one side.

I called his name, but he didn't answer. Then, sheer panic came over me. I remember running over to him and jerking him back up by his shoulders. He was so heavy. To my surprise, when I got him sitting up again, he was still awake. But, he was different. He wasn't himself at all.

Josh's left shoulder was slumped over and his forearm was shaking. The left side of his face looked almost as if the bones had been chipped away - his skin drooped toward the ground. Josh's left side of his mouth had lost it's form and the muscles around his left eye fell down over his cheekbone.

"Is Jim the one that knew it was a stroke?" Josh asked me, assuming that my step-father would be the most educated on the subject of stroke. "No, actually, it was me," I admitted, remembering when I buried my face in my hands and screamed, "Oh my God! He's having a stroke!"
"How do you know anything about strokes?" He asked, bringing to my attention that I wasn't sure of the answer. I hadn't really thought about it before. I guess I just knew.

Maybe it was one of those FAST signs that are plastered throughout the hospital that I'd seen somewhere at some point in the past. Or maybe it was a higher power that was giving me knowledge I otherwise wouldn't have had.

"I just did". Right away I knew what was happening and I called 911 immediately." Josh was upset with me at the time. I remember him looking at me, almost scared by my reaction to his appearance. He shook his head "no" as I dialed the phone. I remember him attempting to reassure me that he was fine. How unselfish, right? As his brain was in the process of shutting down, he was most concerned with calming me. He wanted to make sure that I knew he was alright. He didn't want me to worry. But he wasn't alright, and I had no doubt that what was happening was very, very bad.

Josh continued to layer questions about the night of the stroke and the events that followed afterward. He wanted to know things like, "Was my family at the hospital when they did the surgery?" and "Did the doctors tell you they were going to cut through my skull?"

As I answered Josh's questions and explained the timeline of events that took place in the acute stages of his journey, Josh's eyes were glued to me like a child on his first day in grade-school. He was so intrigued by what all he had been through. Interestingly, he seemed most concerned with the smaller details, having to do with the people involved – doctors, family members, caregivers, etc.

I feel like tonight was a big milestone because this is the conversation I was expecting a month ago. It seems only natural to come out of a near-death experience wondering what happened. But over the last several weeks, the discussion never came. Josh hasn't seemed interested in what he went through. I

119

just thought he must know everything he cares to know, or maybe he just didn't want to talk about it.

But tonight, he showed me that he doesn't know much at all about the stroke. In fact, it seems like everything up to this point is pretty much a blur to Josh.

I feel like tonight was about Josh beginning to wake up - his brain beginning to process interests bigger than the here and now. He's searching for his memory and trying to put together the missing pieces.

I feel inspired by the activity, and I'm glad to stay up late tonight talking with Josh. I can't wait to see what tomorrow brings here at TIRR with Josh.

To end the chat, Josh smiled at me and asked, "Are you ready to pray?" My heart danced with excitement at the suggestion. He heard me explain the terror of his stroke and didn't fear the details - instead he felt compelled to speak to God - and he did it with a smile on his face.

Josh's prayer was touching and when he was done, a tiny tear track streamed down the left side of his cheek. I matched his tear with one of my own - feeling blessed by God that my best friend is here with me tonight, talking to me, praying with me and preparing for a beautiful future that God will provide to us both.

*Wherefore he saith, Awake thou that sleepest, and arise from the dead, and Christ shall give thee light. (Ephesians 5:14)*

------

Dictionary.com, gives the following definition for the word milestone:

"a significant event or stage in the life, progress, development, or the like of a person, nation, etc.: "

Up to this point in our journey, I searched for milestones as future events - happenings that hadn't yet taken place. But as I laid in the hospital chair next to Josh that night, watching him sleep, my eyes were opened to see milestones that had been placed in our path before this nightmare began.

In the Bible, the Lord cut off the Jordan river and commanded Joshua to instruct the Israelites to pick up stones from the middle of the Jordan. He said the stones are to be a memorial for the people of Israel - to serve as a reminder to them of what the Lord had done and to tell their children about it too.

I stared at my purple stone, snug on my index finger, thinking through all of the coincidences that *couldn't have been coincidences.*

I thought about how just two months before, my mom purchased the house directly behind our home - moving from Wisconsin after more than 15 years of living thousands of miles away. *Why did they move here?* It really made no sense - they didn't have jobs here or any pressing reason to just wake-up one day and decide to head back to Texas. In fact, they left my little sister behind at college, which wasn't something I'd ever have expected. *But if they hadn't have done that, who would be watching my children right now? How would I have even managed to make it up to this point without my mother's help?*
Jim and my mom had literally taken over my life for us back home. They took care of our dogs, our house and they took our two kids in full-time, (performing every role Josh and I had).
Jim dropped Josh Jr. off at school each morning and my mother shuffled them back and forth to their practices and tutoring sessions in the afternoons. They fed our kids, did their laundry, helped them with their homework and even parented them with rules and guidelines - as we would do. Was it a coincidence that my mom, (my support system), became my back neighbor just two months before Josh suffered a stroke? Or, was God's hand in that move long before?

Then there was Blessing. How did she know that I would need to be reunited with my faith just before Josh went down? Was it true that God had sent her - as she had told me that night she knocked on our door? What are the odds of a woman I hardly even knew, showing up at our home and demanding that I start a bi-weekly bible study and prayer session routine with her? Why would she offer so much time to me if God hadn't spoken an assignment to her?

Even more interesting was the topics of our discussions. Every single phone call started with, "God gave me this scripture for you." And the scriptures were all on subject of faith and healing. Back then I didn't understand God's mission because he never spoke to me like he had done so with Blessing. But now, I believed that's exactly what had happened. It's as if God had sent Blessing into my life to give me the exact weapons I would need for the battle I would soon face.

My business presented another peculiar set of circumstances. The real estate market in my area was falling into a state of depression leading into 2016. Yet, right before Josh's stroke, I became busier than ever before. I remembered a number of agents calling me to ask, "How are you doing so well? My business is dead." Like someone had opened the gate in the month of March, almost overnight, I was flooded with new listings and contracts set to close in April. My uncle, Bryce had recently acquired his real estate license - conveniently, allowing him to pick up my contracts and attend all of my closings to take care of my customers while we were in the hospital.

If it weren't for these moving pieces, perfectly placed in position prior to Josh's stroke, we would have been out of money already. But God had given us just enough to carry our bills while Josh and I were living in the hospital.

As I toyed with the purple stone around my finger - rotating it back and forth, I could see God's paintbrush carefully drawing every detail that was laid before our season of great trial. I remembered the words of the anesthesiologist who prayed with me before Josh was taken into the second brain surgery - *"It's a miracle that your husband is even here right now. There are only a few surgeons in the entire state of Texas than can perform the surgery your husband needs at this moment. And one of those surgeons is standing right there."*

122

I thought about the missing signature to approve Josh's transfer and the phone call that opened up a room for Josh in the Nuero-ICU. Neha, Kaleb's mom had helped secure that room. She loved Josh because he loved her son, Kaleb. Josh had coached Kaleb in football since the boys were little bitty. *What if Kaleb would've been selected on a different team in that little league football draft 10 years ago?* We wouldn't even know Neha today, and Josh may not have received that transfer that saved his life.

Sifting through a multitude of purple stones that connected perfectly together, I realized that there was truly no such thing as a coincidence - but that all of these moving pieces had been placed in meaningful order by something far greater than me.

It was hard to consider that a situation so awful could be part of God's plan. But, on the other hand, God had given us a support system for our children, faith-based preparation for fighting the enemy and financial stability to keep our home-life afloat while we were traveling through the wilderness.

I could see the stones we had picked up from the middle of the Jordan, without even realizing it yet. We were collecting items of remembrance to see what God had been doing, long before disaster struck our lives.

— *Blessing reading the Bible to Josh in the hospital.* —

Believing in miracles wasn't easy for me throughout my life. Like most people, I'd experienced small things on occasion that seemed supernatural - like the time I jolted my steering wheel to the side and hit my gas peddle, covering both lanes on the busy street in front of the kids school, in order to shield a little boy from being hit by a speeding car.

I had felt another presence taking over my wheel in that split second of decision. But there was no confirmation of my feelings. People would've likely thought I was crazy if I had declared, "God turned my steering wheel to save that little boy." And ultimately, I convinced myself that it was my imagination speaking to me about supernatural intervention.

I guess deep down I had spent my spiritual life in a place of uncertainty, waiting for *the big thing*. Proof that God was omnipresent, forever working in my life was never evident before. And somewhere inside of my beliefs, I had questioned his ability to see me, care for me, hear me and guide me. The God that ran the entire universe must be so busy. Out of billions of people walking the earth at all times, how could he find time for little me?

But now, I could see that he was truly with me - and had been for months, and even years leading up to Josh's stroke. I could see the puzzle pieces of his mystery in our stories. I could see some of the purple stones that we had been collecting all along - I was just too cynical and narrow minded to look for them before - to believe that the creator of the universe could actually be walking with me, writing every detail of the chapters inside of my life.

And in believing that God had in fact been working through our past, my faith was made stronger in believing that it was his hand writing the pages of our future. I felt expectant - a strong sense of waiting and believing for the next chapter to be revealed. I believed in his miracles and had confidence that we would soon see God's best work yet.

*Your eyes saw my unformed body; all the days ordained for me were written in your book before one of them came to be.* (Psalm 139:16, NIV)

Although Josh wasn't able to sit upright on his own yet, his torso was strengthening with every day that passed. OT worked on his balance and coordination. Meanwhile, PT was focused on stretching his paralyzed leg to keep mobility as a future option.

Kyle gave me assignments to work on with Josh when he was resting in his hospital bed. I began to incorporate those leg stretches with prayer. Something about the atmosphere in Josh's hospital room, after we'd read through scriptures and prayed with our hearts, gave me a heightened level of faith in Josh's leg coming back to life.

I started sitting at the edge of his bed each morning after prayer and stretching out his left leg. Then after the stretches I would position myself in front of his foot, hold it up against my hands and say, "Push me off the bed! Push! Push! Push Josh!!!"

I guided his foot each time in the motion I wanted it to go - trying to sense any sort of movement from his limp limb.

Then one morning, it happened!

We had just finished reading a wonderful message about Jesus sitting in the boat with us as we weathered the storm - a message about having faith that he would get us to the other side. We prayed and then I got down in my normal position and asked Josh to push me off the bed.

"Please Jesus give him strength when he is weak," I whispered as I encouraged Josh to push me with his paralyzed leg.

At first, I felt just a faint shove. Then it went back limp. I could hardly contain myself as I jumped up - it was like I'd just seen a ghost.

"Oh my gosh!!! You did it! It moved! Josh it moved! Your leg moved - Do it again Josh!!!"

I propped my cell phone against a cup on Josh's bedside table and then got back into position - capturing video of the big event. His paralyzed leg - the leg that could *NEVER* move again, according to the surgeons, was now moving. *Praise the Lord!*

Josh broke down and started sobbing as he pushed his leg in a forward motion one last time. I cried with him and leaned over to give him a big hug. "He did it baby. Jesus did it. You're going to walk again Josh!"

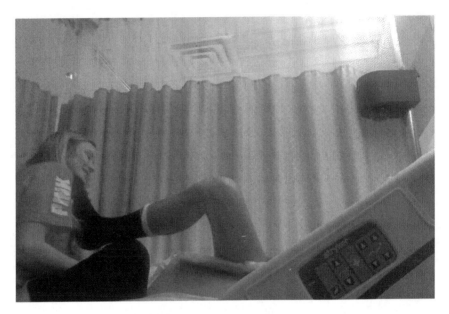

*— This is a screenshot from the video on that glorious morning —*

**Blog Entry - *Josh's Left Leg is Alive***

At 9:59 this morning, Josh pushed me down using his left leg! We have been doing this exercise daily, per the physical therapists advice. I work with him to stretch it out and in result he began having leg pain about 5 days ago.

Today that leg pain, which was an indication that some sensation is coming back to the left side, took a huge step forward. THE STEP FORWARD WE'VE BEEN PRAYING FOR!

To all of the faces we've seen so far in this journey who have doubted what Josh will be capable of, and have bought into Satan's tricks, GOD is bigger than your knowledge, your science and your medical warnings.
God showed me Josh walking with us again. He showed that to me the very night that Satan worked through the tongue of others to inform me that my husband may not live, and if he did, may never have movement on the left side again.

GOD is the only one in control of Josh and HE has spoken and continues to speak BIGGER than all human thoughts, ideas and words, relating to Josh.

If you have prayed for Josh, THANK YOU! If you believed in God's plan for Josh, THANK YOU! If you are taking this journey with us and continue to speak God's name, requesting that he perfect the healing that he is performing in Josh, THANK YOU and PLEASE KEEP LOOKING INTO THE LIGHT WITH US!!!!
GOD IS GOOD!!! Thank you Jesus!

I have to add this..... Right before Josh's leg came alive, we read our daily devotional that talked about being a "GAME CHANGER". It said that God wants us to be game changers, that he relies upon his children who are strong in their faith to encourage other people to renew their faith. It talked about the lie that we live in, thinking that we can live for Jesus on Sunday's, attend church and then forget about him the rest of the week.

The ONLY way to God is through Jesus and the only way to receive his grace is to REPENT. Don't hide from God today. Let HIM see you for all you are (he already does anyway). He knows you aren't perfect - let him into your darkest thoughts, your biggest regrets.. Ask God to fill your heart with his Love and fill your soul with the Holy Ghost! Ask God to make you a GAME CHANGER today - to use you to inspire someone else to be saved by Jesus Christ.

This was our discussion this morning... and then right after our talk, Josh moved his leg. I hope Josh can be your game changer today. Through his strength, guided by the power of God, I hope you will SEE THIS MIRACLE OF GOD and turn to him to create a miracle in you too.

(Here is the video of Josh's legs coming alive in Jesus' Name!) FYI - Video with MACBOOK is a mirror view so it looks like his right but it's flipped. If you notice the PINK on my sleeve is backwards also. This is his LEFT LEG!!!

---

[NOTE]: Video of the first time Josh moved his leg is archived on our website 79ministry.com in the media section.

Perhaps, it was a coincidence that Josh's leg came alive during our morning prayer session. I *knew* better. This was a miracle that I would never be able to deny - a purple stone that I would carry with me forever, filling my heart with assurance that the Lord was with us and delivering us. He alone was our *Master Physician*.

Despite all of the high-tech equipment and impressive resumes of all the doctors and therapists who were guiding Josh's recovery in

TIRR, no movement had taken place in Josh's paralyzed leg during sessions. While I believed that therapy was helping Josh, and very appreciative of the efforts made by all of Josh's caregivers, I also knew Josh's outcome wasn't up to anyone, other than God. And the very big wink that the Lord gave us on this day, was another reminder that he is a merciful God and a powerful God.

*Jesus replied, "What is impossible with man is possible with God." (Luke 18:27, NIV)*

That was one of the most glorious days of my entire life - I'd witnessed a real miracle with my own eyes. I was like a walking-talking billboard the rest of the day as we went through Josh's routine, wheeling him to his different therapy sessions.

"He moved his leg today," I announced to every person that crossed our path - even complete strangers. I was so excited, it took everything I had to contain myself from doing cartwheels up and down the hallways of TIRR.

Kyle was ecstatic. "Josh! This is awesome dude!" He told us that the new movement in Josh's leg would change his strategy in therapy. And he warned Josh that he needed to prepare for some hard days ahead.

"I'm going to start pushing you Josh. We gotta do everything we can in this short time window to get you walking, OK?" Kyle's challenge was music to my ears, and I could tell Josh was more excited even then I was.

That night, we had a special visitor that dropped in once a week, Dr. Prasad, an internal medicine specialist. She was the only doctor that had followed Josh from his very first night in ICU, assigned to manage his blood pressure and medicines.

Now at TIRR, she still consulted with his doctors periodically, and dropped in his room once a week to check on him.

"You have to see this!" I interrupted her mid-sentence as she addressed Josh with her normal greeting - I jumped on the foot of his hospital bed and I commanded Josh to push me off the bed.

As I laughed and smiled ear to ear - so excited to see his leg moving in forward motion so effortlessly, Dr. Presad stuttered, "Do you mind if I take a seat?" She asked as she sat down, almost looking like she might be feeling ill. After studying her face closer, I realized she was crying. *A doctor was crying?*

They weren't actual tears - the kind that flow freely down a person's face, but they were there. I saw the moisture puddling up inside of her eyes and she removed her glasses and rubbed at her eyelids - trying to hide her emotion for me.

"I can't believe it." She finally confessed. "Mr. Manfred, congratulations. You're going to walk again." She announced, in her professional and soft-toned voice.

It was the first time a doctor had delivered a positive report to us. And the irony is, the doctors didn't have any control over this news - GOD had done it.

That night, I meditated on the miracle God had given to us as I laid in the little wooden chair next to Josh's bed, where I slept every night. *God did it! He really did it!* I was simply in awe with the way the Lord was showing us his might. It's as if he was making sure we knew, without doubt that it was *all* him. It didn't happen in surgery or even in therapy. It happened in prayer. No one could take credit for the miracle that we'd seen. It was truly the hand of God upon Josh that had given his leg the ability to move that morning. No doubt about it, all of the glory belonged only to God.

---

**Blog Entry - *It's official Left Leg is Back!!***
So, following our amazing morning with Josh controlling his left leg for the first time since the surgeries, we couldn't wait to tell

his physical therapist, Kyle.   And then of course, Kyle couldn't wait to test out Josh's leg.

Kyle said the left hip and hamstring are firing.  So, his movement is coming back basically at the trunk down.   He did some exercises to confirm that Josh's brain is in fact controlling movement when cued, and he gave me a few new exercises to start working with Josh to help further this along.  Josh is still not firing his quads or his ankles/feet/toes.  BUT, that's all coming!

This is one of the best days of my life.  I've seen the movements on his left side a few times over the last few days, but nothing of this magnitude.  You see, Josh's left side has nothing wrong with it - the injury is to the brain, not the body.  So, it's not abnormal for his left side to move periodically.   For example, when he yawns, his left arm jumps.  Problem is, the injury is to the brain, not his body.   So, what happened today was MONUMENTAL!  What happened today was a MIRACLE FROM GOD!

I'll provide more details as we get closer to our 100% healing.  But just as a small clue as to how big this is.....  Josh is missing a part of the brain that controls movement on his left side, (yes I said missing)...  His brain is re-training new parts to send signals to this leg and move it on command.  This is not some small task.  This is nothing short of incredible, JUST AS I KNEW IT WOULD BE......

Thank you God for your faithfulness and your mercy as you heal Josh and thank you for letting me take this journey with him.  Watching you heal him right before my eyes is the most beautiful thing I've ever witnessed in my entire life. Amen.

By the way, since Josh is showing such interest in trying to use his phone, his OT made him a custom phone holder.  Here's a pic of him sitting outside enjoying the gorgeous day and listening to his music on his phone.  What a Beautiful Day God has Made!

---

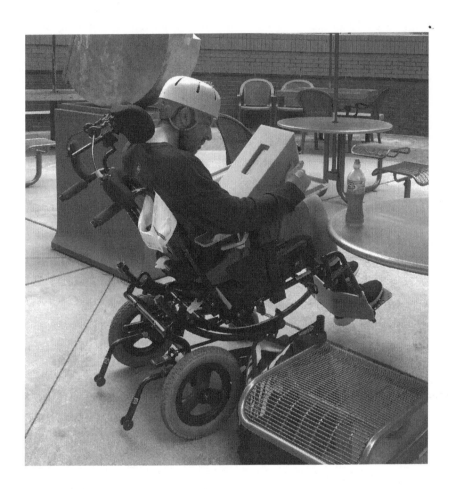

With Josh now moving his leg and a consistency in his blood pressure and medications over the course of the last week, I decided it was time to try and get some rest - *real rest*.  Sleeping on a hospital chair for nearly three months beside Josh's bed was something I'd adjusted to. But I missed my kids and I needed another night home away from the sounds of machines, helicopters landing at all hours of the night and brain injury patients screaming out for nurses throughout the hallways of TIRR.

I asked Vivian if she would stay the weekend with Josh and watch over him for two days. On Friday night she brought the kids up to visit their dad and then we drove home together.

---

**Blog Entry - *Where We Lay...***

I'm laying in my bed for the first time since that night. I look over at his spot where he should be laying next to me, and I feel an emptiness. But then I feel fulfilled at the same time too, knowing that he will be here with me soon.

It will probably sound crazy to most people, but I look forward to life with Josh now, more than I ever could've in the past. I think the world viewed Josh as a handsome, tall guy with a great build and a tough-guy demeanor. Josh was hard to read – somewhat distant and reserved. He was hard to get to know, and I can think of many times in the past when I'd had friends of ours express concern that he didn't like them. It's not that he wasn't a people person, but he just wasn't the relationship type. He didn't care to make friends or to impress people. And because of that he had a tenancy to come off as cold or unfriendly.

The exception – kids. Josh loves children, he always has. He had a special talent in getting through to young people. He could relate to them, and they did to him too. I watched him coach for many years in local football leagues. The passion that he had for those kids was nothing short of amazing. In fact, I doubt they'll ever truly know how much he cared, and how seriously he took his role as a teacher and a motivator. His eyes lit up when they called him "coach" and I could see how proud he was each time a player would accomplish something new - even if it was something as simple as expressing more effort in a drill.

135

The Josh I'm getting to know after the stroke is more of that guy all of the time. The new Josh almost seems childlike. He smiles a lot and really enjoys keeping other people laughing. When the kids come to see him, he puts on a stand-up comedy act for a good 20 to 30 minutes before relaxing back into his mixture of exhaustion and pain medicine. He's overly kind to the nurses, doctors and staff members - even to the visitors that come through to see his roommate. Josh makes it a point to ask everyone how their day is and to shake their hand as they come and go.

I guess somewhere inside of me I'm supposed to be mourning the changes that I've seen. I'm supposed to be upset because Josh doesn't look or act like the man that I'd spent the last 23 years of my life with. The odd thing is, I love him now even more. I don't see his wounds as flaws and I don't see his personality as limited. I see the pureness in him - the innocence. I see a beautiful man that was recently touched by Jesus, and I just want to know him more. I want to be closer to him and be closer to his journey back to divine health.

I know that Josh will walk again because God has shown me that he will. But even if he didn't walk, or even if he didn't fully return cognitively, I wouldn't love this man any less - I love him more.

The bibles says when we care for the sick and for the poor, we are serving our Lord. I feel that part of my mission is to be there by his side as much as I can - to give him all of me through this process as God perfects his miracle. Even as I've destroyed my body and my mind, living sleeplessly in a hospital for over two months, I don't feel frustrated or distraught about this mission. I love this man, and I'm honored to hold his hand all the way to the finish line.

Tonight, I'll lay my head on my pillow in the bed where he used to lay beside me and I will not weep. I will look up to the light and thank our merciful God for the faith that he's instilled in me. I will thank God for not taking Josh from us too soon, and I will feel blessed knowing that Josh will lay next to me again one day. Only this time, I will cuddle against him a little closer than before. I'll talk to him a little sweeter. I will love him more fully because my heart is consumed with Jesus Christ and through HIM I'm able to appreciate Josh more than ever before.

---

Time away from Josh during the few, short visits that I made to our home in order to spend time with the kids, handle our mail and get some housekeeping items done, was like shifting in between two different worlds. I was optimistic and full of faith and joy in one minute, and in the next I was sobbing in my misery.

Home was a reminder of life left behind. Every corner I turned presented me with a memory of our family - Josh in particular.

I remembered him dancing and singing over MaeKenna's speaker and microphone set - center stage in our living room as the kids laughed so hard they curled up in balls.

I remembered him playing ball with our son and his friends in the drive-way. Josh always played nice in increments - letting the kids score on him a few times and then dunking in their faces every now and then. He was so funny - always working hard to keep everyone around him in a good mood and full of laughter.

I remembered the intimate moments between us in our bedroom - the long talks we had together and the way I'd always felt so safe in his arms. Our home was now filled with ghosts of a life that existed only in my memory.

## Blog Entry - *Is it OK if I Cry?*

Breaking down seems to be tied to this home. Everywhere I turn I see him - his clothes, his magazines, his messy drawers, his gym equipment, his scent, his smile, his sense of humor - at every turn, in every room; this is OUR home together. I can't say that I haven't cried several rivers over the last month. But for the most part, the streams of tears are attached to a face that remains composed on the outside. Not tonight.

I cried like a baby, uncontrollably. I yelled out his name and my entire body was shaking like a dryer filled with rubber boots. My heart sank into the pit of my stomach and I felt completely lost until the guilt began to settle in.

I think I've been so strong and kept so focused on my faith that I've refused to allow myself to feel human. Perhaps that is where the line between our spiritual beings and earthly bodies becomes a bit distorted. But then I remembered that God put us here in these earthly bodies, knowing the emotions that he created within us.

I felt him forgiving me, or better yet reassuring me that it's alright to cry. It's alright to hurt. It's alright to be angry and regretful. And I feel him say to me that *he hears my cries and he feels my pain*. Then, once again, I'm reassured that He will not let me suffer forever.

The reality of our lives here can be frightening. The science of trials and the testimonies of victims - they shake me to the bone. I spent several hours on youtube watching videos from stroke survivors. After learning of a miracle drug on a 60-minutes clip, I browsed through the comments and felt myself sinking again.

Post after post shed light on the realities that many of these stroke survivors live with - pain, disability, ab-normalcy, paralysis, speech impediments, loss of motor skills and the list goes on and on and on... My heart goes out to each and every person who is suffering tonight as a result of this horrible weapon of Satan. Sickness is not of God. But as I think through my reality, I remind myself that God is still on the throne. I remember that I've seen his mercy through visions of Josh with this family on a beautiful day in the future. I remember that my mom and my sister Blessing reported that they too have had revelation from God of Josh healed. "He walks", they tell me.

Josh is a son of God with Jesus in his heart. I've witnessed him surrendering to God and calling out his name for help and healing. I've seen the tears bursting from his eyes as he felt God moving his finger for the very first time - just a few days ago as we finished breakfast and prepared for therapy.

I'm not suggesting that Josh is any better than any of those victims who live with the awful effects of stroke, or that God may love them any less than Josh. But I know that we all have our own path and our own purpose that we must find. For Josh, I know that he will fulfill his purpose as a healed man. I know that he is protected by God's word because he BELIEVES. He is a servant of our father and he along with this family will look up into the light every single day, trusting God and praising God before, during and after this miracle has been completed.

*It's OK to cry....* God said to me. This pain is temporary because my God is a faithful God. My God is a merciful God. My God will honor his word and my God will perfect what he has started in Josh.
In Jesus' Name... Amen.

*— More Purple Stones —*

The good news seemed to be pouring in - back to back winks from God graced our days at TIRR. One morning, in particular stood out like a hope-filled picture of what God was capable of. According to the therapists, Josh's arm would be the last to come back - if it ever did come back at all. Most stroke survivors at Josh's level of severity don't ever get movement again. Of course, that's what they said about his leg too. Yet, God had shown the world wrong on that one.

Unlike the leg, this was a brief moment that came and went. Josh wasn't able to repeat the movement. But even though, it was a short-lived victory - it was another purple stone there to remind us that the impossible is always possible with God.

---

## Blog Entry - *Josh Squeezed my Hand Today*

For the first time since his stroke, Josh squeezed my hand today using his left hand. I haven't doubted for a single moment that Josh would not have function of his left side again. Despite the awful warnings from the surgeons that he will have paralysis, or the descriptions given by the stroke team of what it means to have left neglect after a stroke. I believe Josh's left side of his body will wake up. He just doesn't know how to control it yet.

It was difficult to swallow at first. Not only was Josh not moving anything on the left side of his body, but he also was denying that it belonged to him. Josh would literally point at his left arm and ask, "Who's arm is that?" I would try to reason with him and explain that it was his arm but he thought I was crazy. He would respond, "Why would it be my arm? Of course that's not my arm." I fought back the tears trying to avoid showing my concern.

140

Josh's condition caused him to ignore basically everything on the left - his entire left side of his world. If you stood to his left, he wouldn't look at you. Even speaking to him while standing on his left, he would ignore your voice. His eyes wouldn't move to the left - vision only went from center to the right. It was hard to comprehend and terrifying when I asked questions of his doctors. No one ever had anything good to say it seemed when Josh was in acute care. I searched for solutions to "left neglect" and was only given doubt. His docs would say things like, "well, we don't know if it will get better," and "it depends on the size of the stroke, and his was unfortunately very big."

I think the worst was week two in the stroke unit when Josh's nurse was training a new person. He educated her on his "left neglect" right in front of Josh and I, as if we weren't sitting there listening to his words. He explained it to her as if the condition was really cool, "He doesn't know the left side of his world exists. I can put my hand right against his face and he doesn't even know I'm doing it." He smirked, waving a loose hand over Josh's left eye. It's hard watching people categorize Josh as if he's a medical case rather than the great man that I've known for almost all of my life - the father who works himself into an oblivion to give his children a life better than he had - the motivator who dedicated the last 10 years of his life coaching kids. And those who knew him as "coach" will tell you just how big his heart is.

The therapists at TIRR mentioned the "left neglect" upon their initial evaluations of Josh. I don't think I've heard the term again since he's been here. It's like they study a new patient to get an idea of the canvas, then start working on perfecting the painting. Not once has one of his therapists told Josh he has a condition. They just don't view it that way - everything is possible here. Everything can change. That's the attitude that they have and it's certainly the way Josh sees it too.

So, here we are seeing major change in just a short few weeks at TIRR. With my heart filled with hope and faith, I love reporting that Josh already looks all the way to his left side. His eyes move to the left of his head. His hearing tunes into voices in the left side of the room and he is tuned in and even caring for his body parts on the left side of his body. All of these things have happened so fast, it's almost hard to believe he was suffering from such a severe case of "left neglect" over the last month. Today, I'm convinced that it's at least a little bit better - that he's right around the corner from having no more symptoms of left neglect.

Beyond acknowledging the left side of his world, he's now even shown he's capable of moving the left side of his body. In the last 3 days, he's moved his finger for me, he's flexed his left leg muscle while in physical therapy and tonight, he gripped my hand. The doctors said the hand movement wasn't likely "voluntary" but it still gives me hope.

I can't stop thanking God for the progress that we are seeing daily, sometimes even hourly. I know with everything in me that God will heal this great man completely (100%!) and I can't wait for everyone who has doubted him, to see the result of God's miracle.

And all things, whatsoever ye shall ask in prayer, believing, ye shall receive. - *(Matthew 21:22)*

### — *Rex Going Home* —

One of our purple stones came in the placement of Josh's roommate Rex in our lives - a placement that the Lord had appointed for us with great purpose that we wouldn't truly understand until he was leaving TIRR. Rex was only 3 weeks ahead of Josh in his stroke date - and very similar in his stage of recovery.

Talks about Rex leaving soon forced me to reflect on how blessed we were to have Rex as a roommate - to talk to Josh and keep him company. It was comforting for Josh to have a man next to him that knew exactly what he was going through.

I remembered thanking God silently for giving us Rex - a gift that was monumental in our journey and a type of fellowship that had brought Josh much joy over the last several weeks. I assumed that Rex was another purple stone for the purpose of Josh's recovery. I had no idea at that time, that there was more taking place in the unseen.

When Rex, received his release date to return home, a million thoughts flooded my mind. I thought through the idea of what that would be like for us soon - the hopeful visions of life returning home.

Our room had become a busy space with various nurses, social workers and care-givers dropping in at all hours to give instruction to Rex's wife, Lisa.

They taught Lisa how to give Rex his medicines and discussed items for home that would need to be ordered, such as shower chairs, and a reclining hospital bed that Rex could transfer into from his wheelchair.

One night after Lisa left, Rex was more talkative to Josh and I than usual. He bragged about going home, but I could tell he was nervous. "I'm so excited for you Rex," I spoke loudly across the room. "Yeah, I just don't know if I'm ready." He confessed.

Josh and Rex ironically had almost identical right-side brain strokes. Though Josh's was worse - having a second surgery to remove his temporal muscle and a part of his brain, then experiencing a second stroke more than a week later, the two men had very similar symptoms. Rex seemed more alert than Josh - he held conversations well and seemed to process information much quicker than Josh could. But, both of them had complete paralysis of the left sides of their bodies.

"Josh is lucky, he's at least moving his leg. I can't do anything."
Rex continued. "I can't even get myself from the bed to the wheelchair.
I want to go home but I don't want to go home like this."

I tried to be encouraging to Rex - telling him that things would
be fine. I attempted to paint the picture of how nice it would be for him
to be with his kids and his dogs again in the comfort of his own home.
But inside, I knew he was right, and I worried about his transition home -
about Lisa too and how hard it would be for her to move Rex from place
to place. Lisa was built like me - a tiny little thing. I could just see her
straining to lift his body from his wheelchair to the sofa.

"Well, my doctor says I'm ready so I hope he's right." Rex
concluded.

We too had began discussions with the doctors about a possible
release date of Josh from TIRR. However, the conversations were quite
different than Rex explained. Josh's main doctor, and his staff members
kept insisting to me that Josh should transfer to a non-acute rehab
facility. They gave me reading materials and asked if they could set up
appointments for me to visit with other inpatient rehab centers to discuss
Josh's next home away from home.

It was odd that the same staff delivered such different
recommendations to my family and Rex's family, considering the two
men were so closely related in their stage of recovery. In fact, Josh was
maybe even considered further along than Rex because of his leg
movement. Rex, at this point was still completely paralyzed on the left
side.

"Rex? Is another rehab hospital an option for you guys?" I
asked, skimming through the theories that bounced back and forth in my
mind.

"No, our insurance won't cover it."

As I laid in the chair/bed that night I felt guilty about having
good insurance that presented us with options not available to Rex. Even

144

though the doctors had insisted Rex was ready to go home, I could tell that he was scared and uncomfortable with the decision to release him.

On Friday Rex got to leave the hospital for the first time on a field trip out to eat Mexican food. It was a tradition at TIRR for all of the patients who were leaving that week to go out to dinner together.

Josh was jealous - he couldn't wait to get his hands on some non-hospital food. But to his surprise, he wouldn't wait any longer. Rex brought Josh back an enchilada dinner, wrapped in a foil container. It was a very nice gesture. In a way it made me sad - I hadn't realized how close the two men had grown over the last month as roommates. We were going to miss Rex terribly, and I knew he would miss us too.

Friday night Rex was wound up in excitement - talking about everything he planned to do when he got home the next morning. Josh and I traded ideas with him and laughed at his silly jokes. I was glad to see Rex had gotten over the fear of leaving TIRR - and was joyfully welcoming the next big step in his recovery process.

But after we had said our nightly prayers and turned the lights out to go to bed, we saw a side to Rex I didn't know existed.

"I just want you both to know how much you've inspired me." Rex's speech was broken in between loud sobs. "Rex are you OK?" I asked, startled that the joker of a man we'd gotten to know so well was actually crying. He just wasn't the crying type. I knew that about him.

"I listen to you pray every night and I know how much it's helped me." We weren't allowed to move the curtain back between the two beds but I did it anyway - knowing it was important for us to speak with Rex face to face as he cried to us.

He rolled his head to the side, attempting to face us as he continued. "When I was in ICU, I thought I was going to die there. And then I had a dream that Jesus came in a helicopter to get me. I saw Jesus open the door and I was so excited to go with him. I reached out my hand so he could pull me up in the helicopter with him but he didn't take it. Instead he waved at me and shut the door and left." Rex wept louder as he tried to finish his thought - "Jesus left me there... He left me."

I couldn't begin to understand the meaning of Rex's dream. But I could tell the dream had disturbed him deeply. I thought about Rex's heartfelt confession and how he'd said that in listening to Josh and I pray each night, we had helped him get closer to Jesus. It was a beautiful moment - a Godly moment, where I could see the Lord's hand yet again on our circumstances. The Lord had chosen Rex for our roommate, knowing that Rex's talkative personality would bring comfort to Josh. And he had chosen us for Rex too, so that we could minister through outspoken prayers and bible studies. Nothing is by accident when the Lord is on the move.

God is forever weaving a beautiful design in the midst of a broken world. Lives are shattered beyond belief every day, but He never leaves us alone to weather the storm. He gives us fellowship with others and through our unique trials and experiences in unthinkable circumstances, His glory is revealed in mysterious ways.

*Iron sharpeneth iron; so a man sharpeneth the countenance of his friend. (Proverbs 27:17)*

---

### Biog Entry - *Rex Touched by God as We Say Goodbye....*

Josh's in-patient rehab stay was a new beginning from the first day. He met Rex, his roommate who laid in the bed next to him, divided from him only be a curtain. Immediately upon arrival from acute care, Rex welcomed Josh and gave him advice on his upcoming journey through rehab.

Rex was outgoing and talkative - just an all-around good personality and I was relieved that Josh had great company that could relate to what he was going through. It's as if the arrival lifted him to a new stage and meeting Rex was calming to Josh -

146

moving him closer to home and further away from the destruction.

Ironically, Josh and Rex had endured almost the exact same injury - same location of the brain, similar in severity and caused by a clot in the same artery. The two also had the same symptoms. Rex too was experiencing complete left side paralyzation and left side neglect.

Rex seemed much more alert than Josh at first. He was over three weeks ahead of Josh, suffering his stroke the first week of March - Josh's stroke didn't come until the last week of March. It was interesting and insightful seeing how well Rex talked and processed information. His recovery (assuming he was as bad as Josh was earlier on) was inspiring for me, and I think for Josh too.

Rex was scheduled to discharge and return home to his family on Friday, May 6th. The night before his discharge, my mom, Jim, Tori and little Josh visited us in the hospital. They stayed pretty late talking politics and sports with Josh.

After they left, Josh reached out to Rex and asked him if he was excited to be going home in the morning. As Rex spoke, I could hear his voice beginning to quiver. Then in mid sentence, Rex changed the subject and began *thanking* us.

Rex said that he wanted us to know what an inspiration we've been to him. He said that he didn't mean to listen to us, but he had heard us - he heard us praying to God all the time. He heard our conversations day and night over the last 3 weeks. Filled with tears, Rex shared an experience from ICU.

He set-up the story with a joke, saying that maybe it was just a hallucinating from all the drugs the doctors had given him - then

147

he shared with us his dream.    In this vision, or dream, a helicopter had come down to pick him up.   Rex said he was relieved to see Jesus standing inside the door of the helicopter and he reached out his hand to go with Jesus.   But as he did, Jesus waved at him, shut the door and then the helicopter left Rex behind.   Rex cried out and repeated his terror, "He just left me there.   Jesus left me!"   I can't explain the movement in my heart as I listened to Rex share this story with Josh and I - the understanding of revelation that came over me as Rex poured out to us with pain in his voice and tears streaming down his face.

Rex said in listening to us - our faith and the way we pray, that he knows what he's got to do.   He said that his wife is very close to Jesus and he mentioned his involvement too, but with doubt in his words, as if he knew he wasn't close enough to God before now, and he had work to do in his relationship.

My daughter had asked me about Rex last week, after visiting us in the hospital.   She really liked him and always made it a point to join him and talk to him about his day when she was there to see her dad.   On that night of her last visit with Rex, she talked about his excitement to be going home soon.   Rex said he was happy to see his house and his family, but he worried that he wasn't physically healed enough to be functional.   He said he still didn't have movement in his left side, and we could tell he was disappointed in this.   Ironically, this was the same day that Josh regained movement in part of his left leg.

My daughter comforted Rex and assured him he would soon get his left movement back.   She told Rex she was going to pray for him.   His response seemed unsure - like he shrugged her off in a way.   She had called me on her way home from the hospital and told me that it bothered her.   She said she was worried about Rex and she didn't know if he believed God could heal him.   She asked me if Rex had been listening to Josh and I pray. I assured her that Rex could hear us - all the time... Morning and night. MaeKenna said, "I wonder if it will help him being next to you and Dad in that room, hearing you pray."

I feel like that day may have been a turning point in Rex's relationship with Jesus. He was laying right next to us awake that morning, listening to Josh and I pray and discuss our daily devotional. Just as we finished speaking to God, Josh moved his leg on command pushed my body down on the bed using the upper muscles in his left leg. Rex heard us rejoicing, celebrating and thanking Jesus. Rex was there that evening when the doctor visited Josh's bedside and claimed that she now believes Josh will walk again.

I still have the text message delivering the news that Josh had survived the second surgery - the relay of information from the doctors who said Josh should have his memory upon recovery, but Josh would have left side paralysis - Satan's lie.

There is nothing too big for our God. HE is healing Josh completely. HE has given life to Josh's left leg, and HE will perfect the healing in Josh. Aside from just that, our big God is working through us now. He has no mistakes in our path as we have chosen to walk in his light. God chose that room for Josh - he placed us in Rex's life for a short window of time to inspire belief inside of Rex's journey. I know in my heart, Rex will find his own path through God and I am filled with gratitude that God trusted us to do his work in that hospital room - to inspire Rex to reach for HIM.

As for Rex, we will miss our roommate, but we are happy for him that he's now back home with his family. Josh and I look forward to keeping in touch with him in the future. The next time we see Rex, we look forward to seeing how God is working in his life.

We look forward to Josh and Rex reuniting without these wheelchairs one day.

*"Very truly I tell you, whoever believes in me will do the works I have been doing, and they will do even greater things than these, because I am going to the Father." - (John 14:12, NIV)*

OUR GOD IS GOOD! In Jesus' Name, Amen.

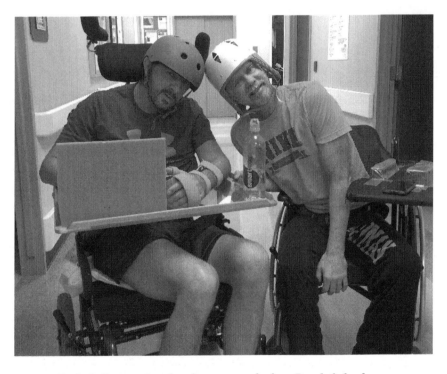

*— Josh & Rex posing for the camera before Rex left for home —*

# Chapter Seven

# *He* Uses the Broken

## Lights in the Storm

The idea of God using Josh and I to minister to others seemed impossible, considering our broken state of existence. I often thought about what it meant to share the good news of Jesus - how to be the light in the darkness for others. In the past, I'd tried to remember to give God the glory for good things in our lives, outwardly. Those attempts were more like afterthoughts on a checklist - at the bottom of my daily priorities in life moving too fast, I remembered Jesus. For example if my kids achieved something awesome, I'd post a picture on social media and say something like, "Thank the Lord for this exciting day." But, now, we just didn't fit that image anymore, in my mind.

Who would want to learn anything from us? Our lives are in ruins right now. No one could possibly take a glance at our circumstances and say to themselves, "Yeah, I want what they have."

One morning while I was standing in the break room, waiting for the coffee machine to fill my cup, a lady with short blonde hair approached me and asked, "How are you doing?"

I recognized her immediately - she was the wife of a patient that lived at the other end of the brain floor at TIRR. I'd seen her following her husband and his therapists into the elevators several times over the last week.

"I'm good. Thank you," I nodded and flashed a warm smile at the lady who wore a compassionate expression.

"Oh… give me a hug!" She said, leaning in to wrap her arms around me.

She whispered in my ear, "I'm so sorry you're going through this, but please know that God is in control. Can I pray with you?"

Something about her demeanor struck me as odd. She was in the same boat that I was in - living next to her stroke-broken husband, who was disabled and bound to the brain injury floor at TIRR. Yet, she seemed almost removed from the struggles that we had in common.

After we prayed together hand in hand, she introduced herself.
"My name is Candice, and my husbands name is Ron," she announced, cheerfully.

"What caused your husband's stroke?" I asked, attempting to make the type of small talk that was normal for us wives that lived in TIRR.

"Oh, we're here because God sent us to pray for others." She beamed, matter-of-factly. I smiled at her in admiration - not knowing how to respond to the cheerful woman. Her faith was like a breath of fresh air - cutting through a place where self pity ran rampant. Wives in TIRR were all part of a club that knew great devastation and loss. Yet this one, seemed to be joyful, despite her circumstances. She was just doing God's work, as she saw it. *How amazing is that?* I thought to myself.

Ironically, the very next morning after I met Candice, I was introduced to Raymond.

------

### Blog Entry - *Meet Raymond...*

God woke me very early this morning. I can't remember the last time (if ever) that I've woken up at 5:30, bright eyed and ready for coffee. What's more peculiar about this is the fact that I've had very little sleep. Josh had a bad night last night, and also a great night. The burning pain that started days ago in his hamstring (which he is now moving), progressed to his quad muscles last night. Then around 3am this morning it moved further to his calf muscles. This was a sleepless night that I welcome with open arms - so overwhelmingly grateful that God is working on Josh through the night to reconnect his feeling on his left side of his body.

Even his Int. Doctor, who had followed him from ICU now believes. She read the reports from the therapist and had sat down with us to watch my videos of Josh's leg moving with a reaction, "Congratulations, Mr. Manfred, I believe you will be walking again." *Hallelujah!!!!!!*

Sorry to get off subject, back to my early morning - I'd like you to meet Raymond. I found him downstairs at the coffee machine, having trouble working the high-tech gadgets. I had trouble the first time I tried to make a cup of coffee with it also. He was very grateful when I stopped to show him and offered to make his cup. We started talking and I learned that Raymond is paralyzed from the waist down.

Raymond is no different than me or you, aside from his commitment to others - Raymond is a vet who spent much of his life in the military. Last June, Raymond went into surgery for a procedure to remove a blood clot from his leg. The unexpected occurred, and Raymond woke up from surgery unable to use the lower part of his body.

Like Josh, and like so many others who never experienced "sickness" before taking a fall, Raymond had no warning that his life was about to change drastically. He had expected to wake up from surgery the same man that he was prior to going in. But, that wasn't in the cards for Raymond.

I told Raymond about how we've been touched by God and he started to cry – I could see the amazement in his eyes – the HOPE in his eyes as he listened to Josh's story. I shared the video of Josh moving his leg for the first time and Raymond was amazed by what God is doing for Josh.

I gave Raymond a big hug and promised to pray for him. But I made sure that Raymond knew the truth – that HE MUST TURN TO GOD HIMSELF – REPENT – BELIEVE! I told Raymond that if he will do that – ask God everyday and believe that God is healing him, he can experience God's mercy.

PRAY FOR RAYMOND..........

Please, while we pray for Josh today, add Raymond to your asking. This is a tender man searching for answers and looking for God's love. Please help me pray to God – ask God to come into Raymond's heart and fill it with his love.

I took down Raymond's number and I will be keeping in touch with him. I know in my heart that this man too can be saved by God's grace. We are all his children and his love for us is beyond our human comprehension.

Thank you God for this beautiful day and for touching my life this morning with Raymond.

*Don't ask God to Bless YOU... Ask God to make you someone else's greatest blessing... and then, YOU will be blessed.*

———————

I didn't think about the conversation with Raymond that day as a connection to my talk with Candace. But later, (much later), I would realize that God had used Candace to begin a process in me - to show me that it's possible to suffer well. And perhaps more importantly, he used Candace to answer the question that I had been asking God in the back of my mind: *How could I ever spread the good news when we're broken like this?* God was showing me that sometimes the broken, are the only ones capable of reaching the broken.

Raymond didn't want to hear a pastor, preaching "God loves you". He wouldn't have responded to a pep-talk from someone loving life - outside looking into Raymond's difficult circumstances. Raymond was drawn to me because I understood his struggles. He knew that the most broken places of his heart were much like the wounds that I carried inside of me too - dreams shattered.

*Was I so different than Candace? Could God show me how to be the light in dark places?* I thought about the conversation we had with Rex the night before he left TIRR - how he'd told us that our prayers and bible studies had inspired him to find a new walk with Jesus Christ. Then I thought about Raymond and his tears of joy as I explained that God is willing and able to pick us up in the midst of our brokenness.

Who was I to promise such a thing to Raymond? How did I know what God was doing with his life, or even with my life?

There are times in our journey when I absolutely knew that I was absent - taking backseat to someone else that lived inside of me. Like a puppet on a string, I surrendered to the guiding hand of something much greater that me, speaking and acting through me. I was learning what it meant to be a vessel of the Lord. He was showing me that he could use me! Even I could learn to suffer well and be uplifting in someone else's tragedy - even in my brokenness.

---

**Blog Entry - *One Step at a time....***
Today is special, like so many other days we've seen come and go over the last 2 months. Today, Josh took his first step without aid. He's on the Vector, (a machine that carries most of his weight from straps connected to the ceiling), and he has Kyle there to lock his knee. But, watch this video closely... JOSH is

putting his left leg forward completely on his own! It's another huge victory for Josh and another step closer to this miracle being perfected by God.

Most people don't consider small victories - we focus too much on the big things we want out of life. And when we get them, there's always another milestone we aim to reach. Celebrating our blessings is corrupted by society's pressure of what is considered "success" - we need a bigger house, a faster car, a prettier face or a more important title encrypted on our business cards.

For those of us who need this man and love this man, those false gods and silly goals couldn't be anymore obsolete. My 14 year old son said a prayer this morning and all he asked of God was for his father to walk today.

I'll cherish that text message from little Josh forever - the excitement he expressed when he learned that God had answered his prayer. And even if Josh isn't yet hopping out of bed to carry-on independently on the legs that God made for him - through our faith we know that the day will soon come. We find patience in small victories - we find love in our hearts and thankfulness in which we praise Jesus Christ, our Savior.

Learning how to eat, talk, think and walk again isn't on the agenda when we plan for our future. Living day by day this journey with Josh, I realize how important it is to slow down. Life wants to pull us in and take us on a never-ending roller coaster ride of "what's next?"...

Sometimes we need to just find peace and take time to reflect on the big picture of who we are and why we're here. I'm blessed to be here right now. I'm blessed to share this journey with Josh and I'm blessed to reflect on our lives with certainty that our purpose is much bigger than what society dictates it should be.

This scripture spoke to me today.... Sent to me from Angela Lambing Kendrick:

*In everything give thanks, for this is the will of God in Christ Jesus for you. - (1 Thessalonians 5:18)*

———————

## — *Miracles inside the Miracle* —

Giving thanks in the storm, was very different than the kind of thanks I once gave to God. It's as if everything I had before taken for granted, was now illuminated before me, as the best gifts life had to offer.

One night I started feeling ill while at TIRR. From an earache, as hours passed a sharp pain began radiating through my mouth and down to my jaw. Remembering my last visit to the dentist, I was quite certain the abscessed tooth that I'd neglected over the last 6 months or more was creeping up to bite me.

Even if I had felt comfortable leaving Josh to see a dentist, there wouldn't be any options for me. It was Friday night. No dental offices that I knew of accepted patients over the weekend.

As the pain worsened I got nervous, wondering how I would stay focused on Josh, dealing with what I knew would be excruciating ache within a matter of time. I had experienced abscessed teeth before - and next to child birth it had been one of the most awful pains I'd known.

Not expecting an answer after 9pm, I sent a text message to my dentist, Dr. Huffman. I'd had his cell phone number stored in my phone after selling his lake house for him about a year ago. He was one of my best customers ever - he and his wife Sherri were just adorable people - sweet and genuinely kind.

As I sat there in the chair next to Josh's hospital bed, realizing that help would likely not come my way, I began to talk to God. I spoke his words from Isaiah, (my number one, go to scripture that I spoke out loud over Josh every day).

"This pain sickness and these symptoms can't take me down. By the stripes of Jesus I am healed! He paid the price and wore my sickness on a tree. In His powerful name I declare healing over this pain in my head."

To my surprise, just as I was finished praying, Dr. Huffman responded to my text. He said he was calling in some antibiotics and pain pills for me at my local pharmacy.

I quickly gathered my purse and slipped on a pair of shoes. Then, I found Jeri, (our favorite nurse), and asked her to keep an eye on Josh while I ran out to pick up the prescriptions.

When I arrived at Walgreens, the pharmacist informed me that they weren't yet finished with my order. So, I decided to shop around until my prescriptions were ready.

I picked up some candy and a few items for Josh - he loved applesauce. When I returned to the pharmacy window there were a few others before me in the line. I stood there listening to the conversation between the pharmacist and a young man, who was explaining his symptoms to the tall woman in white.

At that moment, I realized my pain was gone. Not like numbed down a bit, or reduced to a tolerable level - *it was completely gone!*

I paid for my prescriptions and shoved them down in my purse. But, I never even took those medicines. I didn't need to. The Lord had healed me completely and answered my prayer within the hour of me stating my need.

I'd never understood the difference between praying "thy will be done" and sending out prayers for my will to be done. But as I drove back to TIRR, giving thanks to our Heavenly Father for answering my prayer and manifesting his word in my life that night, I thought hard about the difference between the two prayers. It was a conversation with myself that would continue far beyond the current time.

As far as this night was concerned, I concluded that my faith was the reason the Lord delivered me from the abscessed tooth that night. I gave thanks and Glory to God from the bottom of my heart. And it wasn't all about what he had done for me - it was more about the fact that he had shown me first hand the evidence of Jesus, who is the same yesterday, and today and forevermore. And yes, he heals even today. *Thank you Lord for another purple stone.*

*Therefore I say unto you, What things soever ye desire, when ye pray, believe that ye receive them, and ye shall have them. - (Mark 11:24)*


On Saturday, I left Josh with Vivian watching over him to take my son shopping with me. Josh's therapist required me to buy a different kind of shoe that he would be able to wear over his leg brace. But knowing nothing about mens shoes - I reached out to Josh Jr. for his expert advice. I'm glad I did. My son and I had a great day together.

———————————

**Blog Entry - *God is working in our Son....***
My lil man and I read our daily devotional message together – a routine that Josh and I do at the hospital. Then we prayed together. It's amazing how your day leads off on the right foot when you start it reaching out to Christ.

We spent the afternoon at the mall shopping for shoes for Josh. His physical therapists is requesting a size up because he's casting his left leg for the work Josh is doing to learn to walk again. We also picked up a shirt that reads, "I can do all things.." Branded for Steph Curry. I read recently about Curry's commitments to Jesus and his belief that God should receive all of the Glory for his gifts, talents and success. I'm thankful that this unbelievably gifted athlete is using his spotlight to glorify our Father upstairs and set the example for kids who look up to him all over the world.

As we were leaving the mall Lil Josh said, "All the GREATS do," referring to his opinion that the most elite professional athletes of our time give God the glory. I'm so thankful that he recognizes this.

When Josh was old enough to play sports, we started him in football and baseball. From the very beginning, we saw a spark that inspired us. Josh and I were proud of him, as most parents feel when their kids excel in something. But there was more to Lil Josh than skills – he played with heart. I'm talking HEART that I've very rarely witnessed in anyone, much less a small child.

Lil Josh believed that anything was possible. He was put down at times, as many talented kids are; especially in competitive Texas football. He was criticized by others who said things like, "he's not that fast," or "he's over-rated." He even experienced harshness on a few occasions where adults made comments about the color of skin. Nothing rattled that child. The more he felt attacked, the harder he played – the more he loved the game and the more he loved his teammates. He brought more intensity not only on the field, but off the field in his training. This kid at 6 years old refused to eat sweets and woke up each day begging to run cones and throw a football.

Today, I feel like Josh has a different outlook on what used to be his first love – sports. I see more purpose behind his ideas. I see him understanding that there are no accidents in God and there should never be self-glory. Whether Lil Josh has a future in sports or some other area where God chooses to gift him, I know he's beginning a walk through the light of Christ that will give him guidance and strength along the way.

As we were leaving the mall, we saw a puppy scared to death crossing the busy road. We stopped at the same time as another car and helped rescue the dog. The woman volunteered to take the dog to a shelter where he would be safe. Turns out, she knew us and had been following Josh's story. Her husband was a friend of Josh and I's in high school - small world.

Lil Josh said, "everywhere we go, people seem to know us lately". I believe Josh's story has put our family in the minds and hearts of many people in this community - and I thank God for exposing HIS faithfulness and giving us tools to let others see the miracle HE is performing in Josh and in our lives.

To end our day out, we saw a group of kids on the side of the road raising money for their baseball world series. We pulled into the parking lot and offered them money to help their cause. As we pulled out, Josh said, "Mom, you're so giving. You're just a good person." You know, we don't give to others because we expect recognition - we give because God says to look for opportunities to help others. But in that moment, I realized how important it is for our kids to see us giving. They learn from us, their parents - they learn how to conduct their lives.

God, I ask you to touch our children through us, their teachers who were hand selected by you. As parents, we have a responsibility to lead by example and love others - not to teach hate or judgement of others. God, let us be slow to speak and wise with our words - Let us be thoughtful of your desires for us and realize that by our actions and our words we are inspiring our children to reach for you... to live for you.

God I thank you for this beautiful day spent with my son. I miss our kids terribly, and can't wait until we are all home as a family again. But, I know you will bring good out of all of this and the sacrifices this family is making right now will be nothing in comparison to the blessings we receive as this journey leads us back together at the completion of your perfect miracle.

Father we thank you for letting your son Josh stay here with us - we love him and we need him, and you above all know that God. We thank you for your mercy and your unconditional love as we are not perfect, but we are your children who are saved by the sacrifice of Jesus Christ. It is by the BLOOD OF JESUS that Josh is healed and we will never forget to glorify HIS NAME! In Jesus' Name... Amen!

---

Allowing God to teach me how to suffer well was a new beginning internally. I walked lighter, breathed easier and rested in his constant hand that I could literally feel upon my soul.

Honesty with myself wasn't as difficult as it was before, either. I could look in the mirror and see all the flaws that I carried for most of my life, not feeling the pressure to hide them anymore.

My kids could see this in me too and it felt like there was an unspoken peace that had surfaced between us all. Josh Jr. could call me and tell me he didn't understand his math homework, and instead of yelling at him for not paying attention in class, I remembered all my years of sleeping in math class. The Lord was humbling and teaching me that love can't be attached to expectation - as we were all imperfect beings, falling short of the glory of God every day. We all had challenges and shortcomings, and we all needed love and encouragement, rather than judgmental correction.

He had initiated a process in me of pulling the heaviness off of my shoulders, layer by layer. I didn't feel like I had to be the perfect mom anymore. How could I? I hadn't even hardly seen my kids in months. But there was no guilt in that either, because I knew that I was exactly where God wanted me to be in this season.

What if being the light has nothing to do with projecting a perfect image on the outside, but instead is about learning to love ourselves and others the way God loves us?

I wasn't there to bark orders at my kids morning and night. I had no idea if they were doing well in school, turning in their work, or even attending classes, (although I doubt they'd get that over on my mom). But in walking through tragedy that was beyond my control, I was learning to let go, and let God. I was learning that being a good mother was more about demonstrating love in my own heart, than acting as a drill sergeant that dictated their every move.

I had tried to talk about Jesus to my son so many times in the past. He wasn't interested. He says he believed but he didn't want to hear about how to be a christian - like most teen boys I assume. Yet through watching the Lord work in me by his dad's side, God was showing my son what faith looked like. God had shown my son the power of prayer and even the importance of having a giving heart. It was beautiful what the Lord was doing in our family.

---

## Blog Entry - *Patience*

Ive never been any good at patience. In many ways I've felt this is a positive for me. Having no patience has always made me an overachiever. I want to be first. I don't want to wait for life to take its natural course I want to make it happen now!

Josh and I are a lot alike and he's the same when it comes to patience. On this journey, we are fighting together with that sense of urgency that exists in our personalities but we both know that patience is absolutely required. Just as God is patient with us - watching us make mistakes over and over again. He doesn't grab up us and shake sense into us. He lets us work it out over time - he is merciful.  He gives us free will to learn lessons the hard way, but he's always there with open arms offering an invitation back to him.

Through this experience, Josh and I both are understanding God's patience and giving it back to him.  We are confident that He will sort this out and we must trust Him to completely heal Josh at His pace, never questioning that it will ultimately be done – God's speed.

Still I was full of questions for the PT today.. *How long until he walks? When will he lift his leg and not just push?  When can he move his toes and kick a football again?*  The answers were very gray, as I'd expected.   I know the PT doesn't make these decisions anyway, God is the one healing Josh.  But he did offer an estimated "order" of events.

Kyle says the ankle is always the hardest part.  Once Josh regains full control of his leg, strengthening the knee will be the first objective.   Then, he says Josh will likely be in a cast, then in a brace that keeps the foot and ankle in place.  Listening to Kyle speak I realized that this may be a long process.  And even more importantly, it's apparent that Josh has his work cut out for him as this restrengthening sounds very tough.   Josh was OK with that though and so am I.  Whether it takes a few weeks or many many months, we will do our part.   Josh is definitely working hard to do his part and we will be not only patient with God, but grateful for Him each step of the way.

I think this is an important lesson for us to learn about life because we will always have objectives in the future and also things we ask of God to help us with.  We must know that God is there by our side and when things don't happen right away, we still must trust Him just as he does with us in every obstacle far beyond this one.  That goes for dealing with other people too.

164

To earn our place in Heaven and become more Christ-like, we must learn to be more forgiving of ourselves, our friends and everyone we share this Earth with.

To be honest, patience seems much easier for me today than it has at any point in my life before.  One would think that I wouldn't be able to say that considering our lives remain upside down in many ways.  Our children are living with family, we are living in a hospital room and every part of normalcy that we had in our lives has essentially vanished - the world as we knew it stopped, abruptly.  Yes, I look forward to our family reuniting in our home with the kids and Josh very much - I can't wait to see that happy day.

But, I've found that when I look to God throughout each day, patience just kind of comes my way.  When the Holy Spirit consumes you and God becomes your first priority, there is a beautiful sense of peace that comes over you.  For me, I wake up and look for God to start each day.  When I close my eyes and feel his presence, I am content.  It's a feeling of knowing that I'm exactly where I'm supposed to be and HE has control over my life.

The beauty in this all is that I don't have to worry anymore.  I can exhale in God's arms and know that everything I want or need, including Josh's healing is taken care of.  It's handled.

When you no longer approach life thinking that you have to solve it, patience becomes part of your personality.  Fear and worry drift away into the vapor that we call life, and HIS truth ignites your soul with peace and relaxation.

*Rejoice in hope, patient in tribulation, constant in prayer.* - *(Romans 12:12)*

Most days spent in TIRR were full of optimism - like walking down a path that would lead to a better tomorrow. Yet, TIRR was an *acute* rehab center, meaning the patients inside were all still very fragile. And occasionally, I was reminded of this lingering fear.

One morning, I woke up to the sounds of nurses yelling and feet shuffling outside of Josh's room. I peeked outside the door and saw a group of staff members assisting a pair of paramedics as they wheeled a young man toward the elevator case. I assumed he was going back to the hospital - facing the consequences that the doctors in Hermann had warned me of constantly. They didn't want me to move Josh to TIRR because if something were to happen, time would be of the essence to transport him back to the nuero-surgeons.

After the paramedics disappeared with the patient, I took Josh's water bottle to the break room to fill it with fresh ice.

Jeri, our favorite at nurse at TIRR, was hovering over a cup of coffee with her back turned to me, making sniffling sounds into her drink.

"Jeri are you OK? I asked, placing a hand on her shoulder.

She turned to face me, wiping moisture from her cheeks, then quickly put on her usual bubbly smile. "I'm sorry, I'm so sad for him."

"The guy that they just took away?" I asked.

"He's just a kid. He's only twenty five years old," Jeri wiped at her nose with a tissue before continuing. "His family can't afford to travel to Houston and he's been alone on this journey since his accident. When he got here, he had no clothes or anything. I bought him a few pair of socks and underwear. I could only afford one pair of shorts. But I found a couple of my son's old t-shirts at home and brought them up here."

"That's awful." I responded, giving Jeri a break in telling her story to wipe away a fresh set of tears that were forming in her blue eyes. Jeri had been not only caring for this man as his nurse, but she was trying to sit in for his family too.

166

"Please don't tell anyone. We're not supposed to bring gifts to the patients." She added, looking around to see if anyone was eavesdropping on our conversation.

"Can I help Jeri? If you give me his name, I'll go buy him some things and take them to the hospital."

Jeri scribbled on a small napkin and then rolled it up into a little ball, before handing it to me discretely.

"I wouldn't buy anything yet, Jodi. Wait and see if he comes back."

"You think he may not come back?" I asked, sifting through the unspoken meaning behind Jeri's instruction.

"He's really bad - really, *really* bad," she concluded, as her voice cracked with emotion.

For every patient that was surrounded by loved ones, there seemed to be two or three patients surrounded by no one. It's difficult to go through the valley *with* support. I struggled to imagine what that young boy must be feeling, as he fights for his life all alone. I thought about how scared he must be, with no one to hold his hand and whisper words of encouragement into his ear. And if he doesn't make it, what would his last memory be? Would he remember the terror of doctors speaking instructions to one another as they rushed him into surgery? Or, would he remember the sweet, loving nurse Jeri, that stood in the gap for his family and cared for him in their absence?

Walking back to Josh's room, I prayed silently for that young man. I asked the Lord to give him peace and comfort in his time of uncertainty, as his life dangled by a delicate string of hope.

Unlike the decisions I had made to get Josh transferred to the med center after the clot busting treatment hadn't worked, and the decision to move Josh into TIRR, the decision of taking Josh home that I now faced, seemed to be a lingering question with no clear direction.

I prayed daily for God's guidance. I asked him to give me a sign - and couldn't seem to find one. But as I continued to lay my request down in front of the Lord, I noticed another change taking place inside of me - my desire to pray for others.

At first, I was doing it without even realizing I was doing it. While wheeling Josh down the hallways of TIRR, we would pass other patients and I'd immediately starting praying silently in my thoughts for their healing. Sometimes I would even talk to other wives or mothers in TIRR and ask them questions about their loved ones' conditions. It's as if I was collecting assignments, because immediately after the conversations would end, I went to work praying against those conditions - claiming healing over their lives.

In the past, I would've never taken on such a role - *the prayer lady*. I guess deep down I didn't believe I had the power to intercede for others. But as I became more aware of this new habitual desire inside of me, I embraced it with joy in my heart.

Amazingly, the more I prayed for others, the more strength I found in my own personal requests that I placed before the alter of God. And before long, I quit asking him for signs. I knew the answer I searched for was already embedded deep in my spirit. And even though I hadn't made a decision yet on Josh's next move, I knew that when the time was right, the Lord would give me the answer I needed.

*Pray without ceasing. - (1 Thessalonians 5:17)*

---

### Blog Entry - *Raymond's Purpose*

I ran into Raymond again this morning, outside. He was so excited to see me and tell me that he was making progress. He said that he has some feeling in his legs for the first time in nearly a year (since he was paralyzed last June).

We talked about how he's turning to God and praying to him daily. But then Raymond shared with me a glimpse into his secrets – a past that he's afraid God could never forgive. The truth is, Raymond won't forgive himself. God will forgive Raymond and we know that because he sent his only son Jesus Christ to sacrifice for our sins. Because Jesus paid the highest price, we are saved.

I see doubt in Raymond's eyes in one minute and hope in the next. It's like he's jumping for joy inside at the chance of a bright future. But then, he's ashamed – Satan pulling at his conscious to deliver a lie, trying to convince Raymond that he's done things so bad in his past, God could never considering him worthy.

My question to Raymond was..... Then why are you here?

This opened up a dialogue of change. I could see the light-bulb go off in Raymond's mind as he sorted through potential answers and couldn't find one suitable.

"You have purpose Raymond. God still needs you to full-fill his call. Ask him, believe in him and then trust him." Raymond started sounding off his promises to God. He spoke about how he could testify to his brothers back home and he could change many lives. I felt my heart soaring as Raymond explored possibilities of his purpose out loud.

When I left Raymond at the entrance to the main gym. I gave him a big hug and asked him to turn to the bible and educate his conscience. I told him about Isaiah 53-5 and God's promises of healing. Raymond still thinking about God's purpose for him said, "I know I had a purpose to meet you." I felt tears of joy on the way as he continued. "You saw me and knew I was a lost soul and now you're helping me."

169

The truth is, I didn't know anything about Raymond that morning, except he couldn't work the coffee machine. I didn't seek him out. I shouldn't have even been awake that early on the morning I ran into him downstairs. God woke me ahead of my schedule and then arranged for me to find him.

I had a similar feeling this morning. My body told me to go back to sleep but an aching tooth pulled me from bed and to the coffee machine. Funny, now that I'm back upstairs the tooth ache is gone.

The more I walk in Christ the more I understand there are no coincidences in His path. I've asked the Holy Spirit to guide me – to use me. And right now, as my kids are staying with family, my dogs are in boarding and my husband and I are living in a hospital, I've never felt so content in my life. I am exactly where God wants me to be in this moment.

_____

In the life of Jesus, I recalled a scene where the Lord asked Peter repeatedly if he loved him. Each time Peter answered, "You know I love you Lord," Jesus would ask him the question again. After the third time, Jesus gave instruction to Peter. He said, "If you love me, feed my sheep."

I'd never connected broken things with the will of God before. It just always seemed backwards to me. My carnal mind thought that God had favor on the people who led easy lives - lives of health, wealth and happiness. But in the days that were passing us by in TIRR, a new understanding was upon me.

I realized that God does use the broken things. I realized that in my own pain, I was learning new levels of compassion towards others - people like Raymond. I was also learning that I didn't have to be a life-long Christian or an ordained preacher for God to work in my life to help others.

I learned that even I was capable of feeding his sheep - if only I allowed him to take the reigns and lead me through each moment, he would do the rest. Spending my mornings with Raymond wasn't something I planned at all. In fact, I was certain that the action had nothing to do with my thoughts or even my abilities - it was God working through me with the compassion he was teaching me that would touch that beautiful man in the wheelchair that he loved so much.

---

**Blog Entry - *Do you see his beauty?***

It feels like I've lost track of time living at Josh's bedside. My "real-world" mentality tells me that I'm locked inside of a very, very long nightmare. But that couldn't be further away from how I really feel.

I can recite the footsteps of green colored tiles that lead from the parking garage to the main hall in Jones Pavilion. The textured print of the ceiling is forever embedded in my mind. The sounds of agony, machines and alerted staff play over and over in the background. Visuals of sorrow come and go in new faces, and the sympathy I feel for each of them — especially the ones that load the elevator and hit "Floor 7".

This journey almost seems surreal in that I still sometimes drift off into memories of my life before we got here and then struggle to draw a map connecting that world to the one I'm living in today. There were days I felt detached from myself — weary and weak. Other days I don't even recall — certain that my body was running only on adrenaline. Some of it is a blur and other moments are vivid and rich with meaning that will forever take me to a familiar place in the back of my mind.

My life today may not make much sense on the outside. As I'm stuck between where I came from and where I'm going, I only know that in the present I belong here – by his side. However long it takes for Josh to heal, I will fight this fight with him. And while, I've tried to remove myself in brief moments under the idea that I need a break into normalcy, those are the moments when I've felt my weakest. God wants me here. And, I'm learning more and more, why.

Tonight, I spent some time reading my Facebook wall to catch up on what others are doing. I scanned through political arguments, prayers, announcements, complaints. Nothing has changed. Through social media, the world looks exactly the same as it did before we got here. Yet through my eyes, it seems so far away from where I am, spiritually.

I read the rants from those who think they have problems. Some people are lonely, some are sick, many are angry, some are just bored. And, I remember being one of those people not long ago. I remember getting worked up over a rude driver or someone talking behind my back. I remember feeling anxious or stressed over things that were so unimportant I can't even recall them now – I just know I had those days.. bad days…

I remember getting frustrated when my kids forgot to wash their dishes, mad when the dogs tracked in mud, upset when my husband missed trash day. How silly of me..

I've seen more joy and more beauty in my life over the last 41 days than I can recall in years spaced out over milestones in our lives. And I wonder, how is that even possible? Josh is facing the biggest trial of our lives. I'm supposed to be miserable. And at first I was.

God brought me down to my knees – shattered in a million pieces. I couldn't think. I couldn't see. I couldn't breathe. But as he pieces me back together a little more each day, I think more, see more and breathe more than I have at any point in my past. I find beauty in so many moments – I feel God's presence and relax in his love.

I see hope not only in myself but in Josh – it's in his eyes. He's got fight in him for all the right reasons. He's got ambition and determination, fueled by the second chance that was granted to him only by the hands of God.

This hospital is a beautiful place because we are filled with God's light. His promise. His miracles. They're everywhere but now we see them clearly.

My hope is that God's children all over the world will relax in His love tonight. I pray that we can wake up to a tomorrow and turn to him first and last, worry about nothing because we have faith in his promises and rejoice in everything because even the toughest times can be beautiful if we choose to hold God's hand from start to finish.
Amen.

---

That night, I ran into Bridget, (Adam's wife) in the laundry room. Adam was only 35 - living in TIRR after a horrible car accident severely damaged his brain. Bridget and I folded clothes together and talked about our husbands - how much we missed them *being them*. We spoke about our children and the pain we both felt in wishing we could be with our babies to tuck them in bed and kiss them goodnight.

"Do you have any support from your family?" I asked Bridgett. She told me that her mother had been a huge help and was taking care of her children while her and Adam lived in TIRR. Then her eyes swelled up with tears as she prepared to tell me the rest.

173

"Adam's family has been so horrible Jodi." Her slender shoulders shuttered and I stepped forward to give her a hug. Bridgett cried for several minutes passing and then gathered herself back together again.

"They rarely come to visit him. They stop by, take turns snapping selfies with him to post on their Facebook pages - telling everyone how much they love Adam. Then they rush out and go about their lives." I picked up a stack of socks and helped Bridgett fold Adam's belongings as she spoke.

"What about Adam's mom?" I asked.

"She's the worst. They didn't have much of a relationship before his accident. But that was her doing. She never liked me, so she never came around once we got married." I tried to visualize what Adam's mother might look like. Adam was only 35 - very handsome before the accident, I assumed. Bridgett was simply gorgeous with long black hair and a flawless complexion.

"She blames me for his accident," she whispered, sniffing hard to gather up a fresh wave of tears.

"You weren't even with him in the car. How could it be *your* fault?" I asked, exaggerating my words at the insane accusation.

"I don't know. I guess everyone has to blame someone."

I hadn't had a chance to blame anyone for what happened to Josh. While I felt that the doctors had made some serious mistakes in misdiagnosing Josh's stroke as just a migraine, I'd been too busy with the hectic hospital life to have time to think through the cause of our misery.

I would later learn that blame is a part of the mourning process - a process I wouldn't undergo for quite some time. Even though Josh wasn't gone, those who loved him suffered greatly in seeing him go through such a devastating transformation.

What I learned about a crisis is everyone handles them differently. We all had our different methods for dealing with shock, stress and mourning through tragedy.

Before Josh went down, I thought I had a good handle on who our support system consisted of. Josh and I had our groups of friends, co-workers and family members that were all participants in our daily lives - people that we felt closest to. But when devastation hit us right between the eyes, many of those people weren't there for us at all.

Josh named names every once in a while, asking if specific people had called or sent a card to us. I could tell he was saddened to learn that some of the people he'd felt closest to hadn't reached out to check on him. Meanwhile, we were overwhelmed with messages, flowers, prayers and messages of love sent to us from people we hardly even talked to - some of them complete strangers.

*Maybe it's my fault friends and family had stayed away,* I thought. Never had I invited anyone to visit or given out details of Josh's location. Feeling guilty, I posted an invitation on Facebook and provided the address and room number, where Josh was staying at TIRR.

The next morning i received a text for Anitra, Desmond's mom. Desmond was our son's age - he played on several football teams through the years that Josh had coached. Desmond loved Josh - he looked up to him, like a father figure. And Josh loved him too.

Anitra's message informed me that she had planned to bring Desmond to visit Josh that night. I couldn't wait - I knew Josh would be so excited to see the young man.

Around 8 o'clock, there was a knock on our hospital Room door, Anitra, Desmond and his little sister entered - Desmond was holding a card in his hand.

"Josh look who's here!" I announced, pushing the button that lifted his bed into an upright position.

"Desmond! How are you? How's football?" Josh asked, reaching out his right hand to shake Desmond's fingers.

175

As the young man started to speak, his voice gave way. He stood there, silently sobbing into his shirt sleeve - struggling to catch his breath and answer to Josh's inquiry. But the answer never came.

"I'm sorry.." Desmond muttered under his tears. Josh attempted to make small talk but quickly fell into his own emotional episode.

As they both cried, Anitra pulled the envelop from Desmonds hand and placed in on the table next to Josh's bed.

Before i understood what was happening, Desmond leaned down to hug Josh's neck, and the family of three disappeared into the hallway.

"Please don't let anymore kids visit me." Josh whispered after regaining control of his tears.

"They can't see me like this. They're scared of me. I look like an alien." Josh wept.

Maybe I was so accustomed to Josh's head wounds, that I didn't realize how shocking his appearance would be to others. Josh wore deep scars that outlined the incision area, where the surgeons had entered into his brain. The side of his right eye was sunken in from removal of his temporals muscle, and the entire right side of his head was deflated - severely indented where the skull was now missing.

His appearance was frightening to Desmond. And I felt guilty once again - feeling like I'd caused Josh even more emotional pain by inviting the young boy to visit his former coach.

"You don't look like an alien, Baby." I lied. "You're going to get your skull put back in soon. And then no one will even be able to tell that you went through all of this." I assured Josh. I cried with him until he fell asleep - making mental notes to guard my husband from anymore exposure that would illuminate his pain.

After Josh was asleep, my thoughts turned to my conversation that I had with Bridget. I felt awful for her and the struggles she was facing with Adam's family. It was obvious that Bridget felt very alone through a time when she needed love and support the most. But I was learning through our own set of disappointments that the Lord doesn't always send the people we expect him to. Family and friends aren't guaranteed to be there for us when we need them the most. But, that's OK. Because in those absences, he fills the void with more of himself - and sends others in their place.

Although, I had no solutions or words of wisdom to offer Bridget. I could listen. And sometimes when we're in pain, that's the best gift someone can offer us. God was not only using me to bring comfort to Bridget, but he knew that I would need her too. He knew that long after our days at TIRR, my friendships that I once cherished would be gone. But new ones formed with people like Bridget would flourish into meaningful relationships.

Our nightly talks in the laundry would become part of my routine at TIRR. While it was nice to have support back in our community - people offering prayers and words of encouragement. Bridget had something I desperately needed that no one back home could offer - understanding. We cried together and we prayed together - like two sisters walking hand in hand through the great unknown.

I told Bridget about Desmond's visit and how awful I'd felt when Josh confessed his insecurity with the appearance of his head - stating that he looked like an alien.

"Oh my gosh! I ordered Adam this helmet a few days ago!" Bridget thumbed through her cell phone and then presented me with a skate boarding website. "Adam said it makes him look young and cool." Bridget added, as I searched through the options on her phone.

Josh was beyond excited to receive the package in the mail the following day - I'd paid for overnight shipping on the helmet Bridget recommended.

Not only was he feeling better about his appearance in the trendy skater helmet, but the attention from his nurses and therapists, gave him his mojo back. No longer did he look like an alien wearing a medical hat that appeared to be straight out of a Frankenstein movie, but he looked hip - like a 20-something year old that was headed to the skate park.

The new helmet was most appreciated by his nurse Jeri. She went on and on about how much Josh reminded her of Nate - a young man that she'd cared for at TIRR many years ago.

"You need to read his book. He was truly a miracle by God," Jeri explained behind crystal blue eyes.

Josh picked up a copy of "More God", (Nate Little's book of his survival story through traumatic brain injury), while he was in the library attending a focus group discussion. And that night, Josh and I began a new journey together.

Nate's story wasn't identical to what happened to Josh. But he too had barely lived through uncharted brain surgeries and then attended therapy at TIRR. Like Josh, he was also very young and full of life at the time of his unexpected detour.

As I read through the chapters of Nate's book, night after night, I could see a new shimmer of hope developing in Josh's demeanor. It's like he was listening to his own story - relating to all the deficits Nate described in the aftermath of severe brain damage.

I realized that Josh couldn't fully trust opinions and optimism from those that didn't know his pain first-hand. I believed he could be healed, but I had no knowledge of the misery he walked through each day. Even the therapists who had seen hundreds, if not thousands of guys in Josh's shoes were foreign to Josh - delivering third-party testimonies of hope. But Nate *knew*. He'd been there - literally he'd walked through the darkest hours of traumatic brain injury and he lived today to tell his testimony of God's miracles on the other side of healing.

It was a monumental milestone for Josh to journey through the story of another man who had experienced his pain - a man that understood Josh's feelings in the nightmare he lived inside of. And as we read that book, my understanding for purpose in the broken reached a new level once again.

*Blessed be God, even the Father of our Lord Jesus Christ, the Father of mercies, and the God of all comfort; Who comforteth us in all our tribulation, that we may be able to comfort them which are in any trouble, by the comfort wherewith we ourselves are comforted of God.*
*- (2 Corinthians 1:3-4)*

## — Oh, Father —

Josh spoke about the kids to anyone and everyone who would listen. His therapy sessions in PT and OT were passed with stories about our children. While they stretched Josh's limbs and hooked him up to the e-stem equipment, he bragged about Josh's sports achievements and our daughter's beautiful voice. He'd always been so proud of Josh Jr. and MaeKenna. But now, more than ever he treasured them dearly.

To me, I saw a man who missed his life so deeply, it was the only way to feel a sense of normalcy - sifting through memories and sharing tales of our lives back home.

Every night MaeKenna conferenced us on video chat. Her and Josh Jr. took turns telling us about their days at school. It was without question, Josh's favorite part of his days at TIRR. As soon as he was finished with his last therapy session, he always asked for my laptop. "Make sure it's charged so they can call," he would instruct.

One night, MaeKenna called from a different setting. She'd propped her phone up on one of the bookshelves in our library and waved at us hands-free with a huge smile on her face.

"Yall ready? I have something to show you dad! I wrote you a song..." She beamed, as she took her seat in front of the piano and adjusted her microphone to her lips.

Before MaeKenna was half-way through the first verse, Josh was weeping over my keyboard. I was crying too. The song was just beautiful - retelling the story of our faith filled battle in ICU room #79.

It was a purple stone moment, we would never forget.

Here are the lyrics to MaeKenna's song that she wrote for her dad and performed for us that night over video chat:

*Nothing feels the same*
*and I want to scream out your name*
*But I know that you can't hear me yet*
*But you will, because*
*Father, it's not your time*
*Our Father is by your side*
*And he's healing your shattered wounds*
*Because Jesus died for you..*

*It's so hard to be strong*
*I just want you to come home*
*I know that you can't be with me yet*
*But you will.*
*Because Father it's not your time*
*Our Father is by your side*
*And he's healing your shattered wounds*
*Because Jesus died for you..*

*The doctor said to say goodbye*
*But Jesus said Satan lies*
*The faith that carried me through that night*
*Is leading you through this fight*

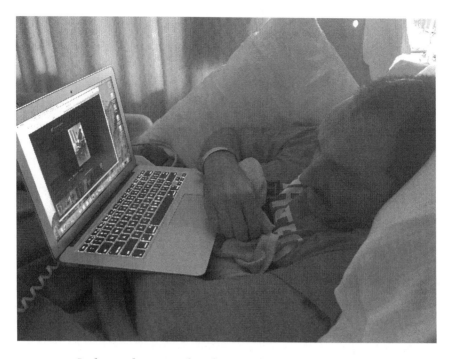

*— Josh watching our daughter perform her original song she'd written for him, "Oh Father" —*

*[Note]: We have placed a video of MaeKenna performing this song on our website, www.79ministry.com. Please feel free to navigate the media section to watch our daughter perform her song, "Father".*

## Afterthoughts...

In many ways, our journey through TIRR felt empty at times. Progress was slow as the weeks passed us by and Josh's healing wasn't what I had expected upon our arrival. Yes, we had celebrated great victories. But in the grand scheme of things he was still very broken - no where near a state of independence that would allow him to return to a normal life back home.

Yet, God was teaching me that our journey wasn't all about us - not even all about Josh. God was teaching me that he uses the broken things to change hearts and to build our faith in him.

From showing us how to pray faith-filled prayers, to showing us the beauty of fellowship with others who were in the midst of a storm. Even our broken lives could serve a great purpose in the moments appointed by God.

Through pain, the Lord had cracked our hearts open and allowed us to feel true compassion for others. Through pain, he was changing our children's hearts too.

Out of all the moments I had cherished throughout mothering a precious little girl, nothing in my memories held a candle next to that song my daughter wrote for her daddy.

And my son, who now knew how to pray to the Lord and seek the Lord, had never made me feel more important and accomplished as a parent. When he spoke the words, "Mom you're such a good person," he wasn't fluffing up my ego. Josh Jr. was witnessing the living God working through the life of his mother, as I surrendered to the Lord's will and smile even through the pain.

God was showing us that we weren't alone. Through people like Bridget and stories like Nate's, he was revealing the important purpose that we all have in our trials - to endure them by his power and then testify to others.

God was teaching us how to suffer well. He was showing us purpose in our lives beyond us - it was all about him and his beautiful creation of moving pieces that alter and perfect our paths for the glory of his name.

In the book of Proverbs, the Bible says, *The fear of the Lord is the beginning of wisdom: and the knowledge of the holy is understanding, (Proverbs 9:10).* I had never been taught to fear the Lord. I'd been taught that the Lord was my savior and my friend. *How could these two conflicting ideas become one?*

As the purple stones of our journey became more evident to me, I was learning that the Lord is in control of all things - that *coincidence* was a lie of humanity - a philosophical error. I was learning that God draws us out, to bring us closer to him, and only in my brokenness could I have seen these truths.

Through the stories of Rex, Raymond, Candace, Bridget and even Nate, we were learning a side to life we hadn't known before. It was as if a veil was being lifted from my eyes and I was beginning to not only respect and fear the Lord, but I was also beginning to respect his process.

*My brethren, count it all joy when ye fall into divers temptations; Knowing this, that the trying of your faith worketh patience. - (James 1:2-3)*

# Chapter Eight

# *Josh* Will Walk

## The Countdown Begins

Rex's departure was a passing of the baton to Josh and I. Immediately after he went home to be with his family, we were given a projected release date and placed in line for planning and training. I had made so many decisions up this point on Josh's behalf. But now, Josh was more alert and even opinionated.

His therapists took turns spilling out all of the benefits in transferring to another rehab facility. They gave us brochures and shared testimonials from the three choices at hand - a place in Galveston seemed to be the favorite of all three. Josh was not on board at all.

"I'm not going to another hospital." He concluded. And even in the private conversations between us two, I could sense his frustration with the worn out topic. It was his choice and he'd already made it, as far as he was concerned.

"Are you sure he's in his right mind?" Josh's father, Jim, asked me, as we talked in the hallway at TIRR. I knew Jim wanted the best for his son, just as I wanted to make sure Josh had every opportunity to get back to health. I wanted him to regain his life and become independent again. But, I also felt great compassion for what the decision would mean for Josh, mentally.

He'd been through so much. We both had. When we were alone sometimes, Josh would confess to me how tired he was. "I feel like I'm in prison. Jodi, please just take me home," he begged. How could I be so cruel to deny Josh an opinion on his own recovery? At the same time, how could I let him make a big mistake?

"He's not ready. He needs more therapy." Kyle was talking to both of us while operating the motorized bike that was attached to Josh's left leg. If anyone would convince Josh to transfer to Galveston, Kyle was the guy. "I'm not going to Galveston." Josh said firmly.

"Kyle if he's not ready to go home, why can't he just stay here at TIRR?" I could tell my question was uncomfortable, based on Kyle's expression on his face. He seemed to be searching for careful words.

"Insurance. You'd have to talk to his case worker." Kyle wanted to say more, I could sense it. But, he didn't. I remembered Rex's comment about insurance - implying it was the reason that Galveston wasn't an option for him.

Josh's case worker presented an alternative option to Galveston - the TIRR Challenge Program. The outpatient therapy option would be rigorous and non-stop, requiring me to drive Josh to and from TIRR three to five days a week, depending on the TIRR Challenge recommendation. The good news was, I could care for Josh at home in the evenings and over the weekends, making sure that his exposed brain was kept safe from harm. The bad news was, I would have to manage Josh's needs at home all by myself.

Members of Josh's family continued to express opposition to the idea of Josh going home, afraid I couldn't handle him. And some of the communications were intense, as Josh delivered stern refusals to each attempt made in motive of convincing him otherwise. There were times I felt caught in the middle of it all - and it was stressful.

I cared deeply about the opinions of his loved ones. But at the end of the day, the weight of the matter was on my shoulders. I was the one that would have to sign off on our release plan and either move to a hotel in Galveston - extending our absence from our children's lives, or go home and weather the difficult task of keeping up with the outpatient schedule and caring for my disabled husband alone. He was my husband and the father of my children - broken or not, he always would be in these roles. His outcome was a vital part of my life. I assumed his family would help me out in taking care of Josh as much as they could. But I knew that I would ultimately wear the title of *primary caregiver* over Josh's life until he was able to be independent again.

And while the decision was mine, it was also his, (at least in my mind). I realized he wasn't capable of thinking to the capacity he once could. But even though he may not have known what was best for him at that time, he did know how he felt. Josh may have been limited, but he was still in there. He still had a life to live and it was *his* life, which I respected more than ever before. Josh desperately wanted to go home.

---

**Blog Entry - *The Enemy Looks for Open Doors.***
***God Closes Them.***

When you think about going through a tragedy, you assume that everyone will come together with love and support to help you through the storm. Unfortunately, the enemy is always on the prowl looking for cracks and crevices - when he can't get to you, he tries to hitch a ride with those surrounding you.

Tonight I'm giving a situation to my God that is causing stress, disagreements and fear. God will make sure that nothing working against my family will prosper. My God is amazing!

Josh and I attended Church this morning. Immediately after walking out of the service, Josh gained new movement in his left leg (again). It seems with everyday passing he's gaining something more. God is fully engaged and I praise him!!!

After church, Josh's Dad, Connie (Jim's girlfriend), and Jason & Jess came by to visit for awhile. Josh really enjoyed their company - he was glad to see them.

It was late in the day before Josh's blood pressure finally came down. We spent the rest of the evening reading "More God." I think I've nearly lost my voice. We literally read through over half of the book today. Every time I went to set it down for a break, Josh would say, "Keep reading! This is a good part!"

It's truly inspiring to go through the story of Nate with Josh. As we read, both of us share tears in the hard parts and smiles in the uplifting ones. It's amazing how similar their stories are in so many ways.

Like Nate, I know Josh's situation has impacted many lives. I know God is working through Josh to encourage others and I know that the outcome to this all will be beautiful, as is God's perfect plan.

You know what else I know?... I know Josh will walk! I know this miracle that my Heavenly Father is completing will be done. I know that everyone following this story who is skeptical will be faced with a reality that God is in control. He is our Healer. He is faithful and He does not fail us!

Thank you God for giving me the knowledge to identify the tricks of the enemy and the strength to overcome my humanly instinct. God I know that I'm not perfect, but God I'm thankful that you have the perfect love. God I surrender to you and ask you to fill my heart with your love and your guidance. Thank you God for all that you are doing in our lives. Thank you God for healing Josh as I know that it is done.
In Jesus Name. Amen.

---

After praying and sleeping in the perfect peace of Jesus that night, I woke up with my decision. I was going to take Josh home, even though going home seemed impossible. I wasn't ready to take on the high-level of care Josh needed and Josh certainly wasn't ready. At this point he was still not able to sit up on his own, dress, shower, or even eat on his own. Yet, in my heart I knew it was the right decision for Josh. In response to my decision, TIRR gave Josh an extra week for extended training - and provided an absolute release date of June 3, 2016.

"There are psychological benefits to being back at home," Dr. Joseph explained - supporting my decision. "But it will be very hard on you, his care-giver." If I was the only one who would experience sacrifice in taking Josh home, I was up for the task and determined to make it work.

*Josh Will Walk* was a theme I initially started after arriving at TIRR. I confessed this hope by creating a daily blog and naming it *Josh Will Walk*. Even though Josh was now moving parts of his leg, he was nowhere near walking. In fact, the closest he had been to actually walking was riding on the vector harness that hung from the ceiling in the main gym. The vector held over 70% of Josh's weight for him - allowing him to focus on learning to take steps, without bearing the heavy load of his body. The harness also kept Josh safe from taking a fall.

Josh walking again, I fully believed would become a reality one day. But in preparing my mind for what going home might look like, walking seemed to be the only answer. I *needed* it to happen now.

I couldn't handle Josh on my own. I'd barely been able to complete wheelchair transfers. And getting him into my car would be simply impossible.

Yet God was telling me that home was the answer - I knew it deep inside of me. So, I convinced myself that God must be up to something new in our countdown to leaving TIRR. *God was going to stand Josh up and walk him out of this place,* I told myself.

188

As a gesture of my great faith in the Lord's ability to do the impossible once again, I launched a seven-day countdown to Josh's departure on my blog. I posted prayers, scriptures and claimed with all my heart that Josh would walk out of that building.

---

**Blog Entry - *He will walk....***

The last week in particular has brought about many decisions and a weight of stress as we sorted through opinions and options. In learning that Josh may be eligible to transfer from here to another inpatient rehab facility, Josh's attending doctor strongly recommended departing for Galveston this week. The move would come premature to Josh's upcoming surgery to replace his skull, and it would extend Josh's absence from home another 30 days at minimum.

Josh quickly said, "no" to the idea. But after some persuasion from his family and his doctors he said he would consider it - but only after he gets a break. He is simply exhausted of hospitals and staring at fluorescent lights trapped inside four walls all day. I get it. I understand him wanting a break.

The decision to go home on the new release date of June 3rd has helped me to focus again - to turn to God and ask him to take the stress from my shoulders. Last night I could feel the winds of change in the air. I could feel God reaching out to me and calming me with his embrace.

We didn't sleep much. Josh's new roommate is having some breathing problems and staff are in-and-out every 5 minutes it seems. Josh tossed and turned as the bright lights turned off and on repeatedly throughout the night. Around 3 a.m., I heard him moving around a lot, so I got up to check on him. Josh was literally sideways in his bed with his left knee up in the air and his left foot pushing against the side of the bed. I notice involuntarily movement sometimes when we transfer from his chair - where the left leg follows the right and he pulls it up, without him knowing he's doing it. The doctor said this is sometimes associated with a disorder where muscle memory is in tact, but movement on command is not.

When he was awake, I told him about the movement overnight and asked him to really try his hardest this morning when we did our leg stretches. We prayed. We did our daily devotional. And then, he powered up his quad for the first time - completely locked the leg, and the muscles were visibly flexed from his knee up his thigh.

It may seem unreasonable to say Josh will walk out of this place in less than a week. But nothing is too big for my God. I believe HE will do it. Amen.

---

With only a few days to prepare for our final move from TIRR back to our home, at last, I was excited and yet terrified at the same time. Josh was in a full-care system. He had technicians that moved him, bathed him and changed his adult diapers. He had nurses that visited him like clock-work, administering over 30 different medications that had to be taken at specific times. He had therapists that not only worked with him daily, but they brainstormed issues constantly - like addressing the ever changing pains in his left side. They created harnesses and slings to keep his left shoulder out of pain and they introduced ways to help him complete tasks, like attaching his cell phone to his wheelchair tray.

Doctors oversaw his care, revising his medicines and running tests, as needed to monitor his blood pressure, among other levels that were unpredictable and often not regulated correctly by his injured brain. Josh even had a nutritionist that worked with the kitchen at TIRR to insure

Josh's diet was suitable for his recovery. As Josh's needs changed sometimes daily, he had a full staff of experts around him to respond accordingly.

I didn't even know how to cook, much less act as his nutritionist, nurse, therapist, doctor and technician. Yes, I was terrified of what challenges laid ahead of us in going home.

And as if we needed anything else added to our plate of worry, Josh's right eye had started swelling again.

---

**Blog Entry - *The Glass if Half Full.....***

Someone close to me presented the "glass half-full" concept when I was a kid. I remember listening to him in amazement at how easy it is to possess a completely opposite outlook on the very same subject, all dependent upon how you choose to see it. I've thought a lot about perception recently, mainly because having faith requires me to do so.

If I trust God to heal Josh and to put our lives back together again, I can't focus on the bad things, believing what my eyes report to me. I remember when I first saw Josh after he was brought back from surgery. For a brief moment, I struggled with the idea that it wasn't him laying in that bed at all. It certainly didn't look like him. It's like I wanted to reach into that wounded body and pull him back to the surface. I wanted to see Josh, talk to him, laugh with him. I wanted to hear his voice and see the dark golden rings that line the pupils of his eyes. But I couldn't.

*"For We walk by faith, not by sight." - (2 Corinthians 5:7)*

It's not always easy to deny what you see. When Elijah told Ahab to look for water, he knew his prayer would be granted by God. And even though Ahab came back time and time again to report to Elijah that there was no water, Elijah didn't give up. He kept praying - he believed that God would deliver and his faith in what was not yet done was bigger than the reports from Ahab. He sent Ahab seven times, and in the midst he kept praying to God - Elijah was sure that God was going to make it happen. And HE did.

Just like the water that didn't yet pour from the sky, I saw the image of a man that was far from the Josh I know and the Josh I wanted to see. And just like Ahab's reports, I too had heard reports that were hard to swallow - reports full of doubt and defeat. But I know that my God can do anything. So, I closed my eyes and I reached for him and when I did, HE gave me the vision that I longed for - the visual of a healed Josh.

Sure, when I saw Josh again with my carnal eyes, the man on the hospital bed was unchanged in that moment. But I chose not to believe what I saw in the present; I chose to believe what my God will do. It's a battle I face each day now to hold onto hope. But I'm winning the battle. I'm choosing to "walk by faith, not by sight."

Today, I feel a lot like Elijah did, I would imagine. I've seen miracles and I thank God completely for each victory that I'm able to witness on this journey. However, I know too that the finish line is still far away from where we are today. So, like Elijah, I keep praying… I keep believing and I keep my faith in what God will deliver to me soon. I wait patiently for God to complete this miracle, but I expect fully for it to happen; and I believe that it will.

One of the things I truly appreciate about this hospital is the positive spirit of those working with Josh. Since we left the main campus, I hadn't heard anymore about how "bad" it is. No one has spoken to us about the injury, the potential setbacks or possible disabilities. It's been a, *"the sky is the limit,"* kind of approach to recovery and Josh has taken the lead and progressed more each day.

When I learned that we may have an issue due to the unexpected increase in swelling in his head, I prayed and held onto the vision God had given me back in ICU. I commanded the enemy to get lost and I reminded myself of the battles we've won so far. Still, I fasted all day, awaiting results from the CT Scan. I focused my attention on God and surrendered myself to his comfort - asking him to be in full control and trusting him with the outcome.

The doctor that delivered the news is filling in for Josh's primary doc this week. She went through the results with us and said they were very reassuring. Specifically, she said both the bleeding and the swelling were very close to being resolved. She said all is healing nicely - while there was some softening of the damaged brain tissue, she said that too is completely expected at this point in recovery.

She looked at him for a moment with a puzzled expression. Then she said, "I have to admit I'm shocked after seeing the scan." I asked, "What do you mean?" She said, "It's just that he's doing so well - I'd never expect that from the picture." I felt my heart drop a little, still trying to sort through what she was getting at. She had just said that *everything looked great* prior to these comments.

"But I thought you said everything looked good," I insisted. "Yes, it does. I just had no idea how severe his stroke was. It's amazing he has recovered so much function."

This was the first time since the stroke unit that someone had mentioned the severity of his injury. While it was alarming in a way to be reminded of the scientific views of what the doctors expected of Josh, it immediately prompted the phrase, "Thank you Jesus," to roll off my tongue.

There is nothing too big for our God. I know the doctors will continue to be amazed as God defies their medical logic and heals Josh completely. Our Glass Is Half Full... In Jesus' Name. Amen.

———————

With the swelling scare behind us, (just another bump in the road), our focus was back on preparing for home, and time was running out.

Kyle asked us to meet him at 2 o'clock outside of the front entrance of TIRR, to teach me how to work on transferring Josh into my Yukon. Understanding how difficult it still was for me to move him from a bed to a wheelchair, I was nervous about car transfers. But, I would have to learn and learn quick.

We waited at the front entrance of TIRR with my Yukon running. I'd pulled Josh's wheelchair over to the passenger side door and moved fast to clean up the trash and clothing items that covered the leather seat we'd be working with.

We briefly tried transfers before, and did pretty well. But, I'd relied heavily on Kyle's assistance with each step. Josh wasn't able to stand on his own - meaning I had to somehow shift this 6'2, 220 lbs. man from a low-laying wheelchair, through a door, and onto a raised seat that was almost level with my chin.

We tried at least 10 times - failing with each attempt. Something was different and nothing we tried seemed to be working in our favor.

Kyle stepped in to keep Josh from falling to the ground, over and over, as I wrestled with all of my might to bring Josh to a standing position.

"Don't worry we'll try again tomorrow." Kyle assured me, wearing an expression that defined worry. He knew there was no way my little

194

100 lbs. frame was going to be able to get Josh into that truck by myself. I knew it too. Home was starting to seem like a really bad idea.

---

## Blog Entry - *Defeated. Blessed!*

Today in physical therapy, Kyle decided to spend just a few minutes working on our car transfer again in preparation to go home. Last week, Josh and I had mastered the difficult move with Kyle's help. We were the perfect team - he would stand up with his right leg while I supported his left leg and swung his hips to the side. Then once his hips were lined up with his bottom to the seat, I lifted his left leg, he lifted his right side, and then pulled his legs around in front of the dashboard. Considering Josh has gotten much stronger since last week, I expected the car transfers today to be a breeze, and so did Kyle. I had hoped this time, we would be successful without needing assistance from Josh's PT.

It didn't go well at all. In fact, I almost dropped Josh at one point. We tried over and over again and nothing was working right. Kyle, who's very strong, took over for me in attempt to figure out the issue. He too struggled with Josh and then wrestled his left leg, which wouldn't bend. I'd never seen Kyle so flustered. He said, "Josh I can't bend your leg against your power pushing it straight." Josh just answered complaining that his left leg was hurting badly. "It's on fire." We both dismissed his complaint assuming the usual nerve pain was to blame. Kyle suggested we take a break and give his body a few seconds to stop having spasms (nerve pain side effect).

For a full hour we tried over and over to get it together without resolve. Until finally, I almost completely lost Josh when a powerful force pushed his body weight away from me. He was supposed to be coming toward me - he leans forward and stands up with his right leg… But something was forcing Josh's body the opposite direction half way through the motion. Kyle assumed Josh was turning his hips. But that didn't make much sense because twisting his hips with all of his weight on one leg wouldn't push his weight the opposite direction of the place he'd came from. It just made no sense.

I felt hot tears entering my eyes as I realized I was in big trouble. I have only two days until Josh is released from this hospital to go home with me. And once there, I have to transport him back and forth to therapy three times a week and to all of his doctor follow-ups. As of now, I don't even know how I'll get him home, much less back in the car again to go about our lives.

Sitting in the wheelchair assessment, a light-bulb went off in my head. His left leg was pushing the weight backward! I mentioned it to his therapist in the form of a question and Josh interrupted, "It's because I'm using my left leg." His therapist looked at him with raised eyebrows. "Josh, you could feel your left leg pushing when you stood up?" "Yes, and it hurt really bad," he confirmed. *Wow!*

I don't know how it will go tomorrow as we will have to figure out another method, scheduled to practice car transfers again. But I do know, HE is doing it. God is filling that left leg with the strength to push and hold Josh's body weight.

How can I be frustrated and overwhelmed with worry over the issue of not being able to load Josh into the car when our Amazing God is giving me a sign that Josh will be standing on his own soon? I can't.

Nothing is too big for our God. He will provide for us the way and I know in my heart it will look nothing like the original one-legged transition we had practiced before.

Thank you God. You are Amazing.
In Jesus' Name... AMEN!

---

After physical therapy, I pushed Josh back to his room to prepare for his dinner field trip - the first time ever he would see the outside world since his stroke. The farewell group had decided upon Italian food. Josh had bragged about it for days - telling all of his therapists that he planned to order everything on the menu. He hated hospital food - so this was a very needed treat for Josh.

I wasn't allowed to go with him.. So, I decided I would spend my free time shopping for items we may need once we were back home.

I took pictures and video of Josh loading into the van - like a mother sending her child off on his first day of school. I cried in the same way, feeling nervous, yet so excited for this big milestone.

When the bus was loaded with all of the patients attending the dinner, I jumped in my truck and headed toward Ross. Once at the store I loaded my cart with things for Josh. I bought him sports bottles with easy to push button-tops. They would allow him to keep a drink by his side without it spilling, while accessing the lid with one hand. I bought him a few hoodie shirts - he always complained that he was cold since his stroke. I also picked up a carrying case for his cell phone that would attach to his wheelchair by magnet. Finally, I bought him a few packs of clean underwear that were large enough to go over his diapers.

I made a quick stop through a drive-thru to buy myself lunch, and then parked my truck outside of the Italian restaurant, within view of the TIRR van. The anxiety was killing me - wondering if Josh was doing alright without me there to help him inside the restaurant. I worried about him choking, (I had been cutting his food into tiny pieces before each meal). I worried about someone walking by and bumping into his head. Even though he wore a helmet to protect the exposed part of his brain, where his skull had been removed, I questioned if it would provide any real protection against a blow.

That was one of the reasons I had felt uncomfortable with the idea of sending Josh to Galveston. The rehab unit there didn't provide 24-hour nurses that would watch over Josh through the night. Also, they wouldn't allow me to stay with him. If he were to roll off his bed or accidentally pull one of the machines on top of him, even a small blow to the head could be fatal.

I looked around the empty parking lot, realizing I was the only family member from the field-trip bunch that was literally stalking the TIRR dinner outing. And it was a little unsettling to admit to myself that fear and anxiety were still very much attacking my thoughts. I honestly couldn't help it at times. After witnessing how fragile life is, and in knowing how fragile Josh's condition was, even to this day, it was hard for me to let him out of my sight. I had been so close to losing him once, and I couldn't bear the thought of ever going back to that place again. *But, is it up to me? No. God owns everything, including Josh's life.* Choosing faith over fear, I forced myself to start my car and head back to TIRR - aborting the stalking mission and trusting God to keep Josh safe.

*For God hath not given us the spirit of fear; but of power, and of love, and of a sound mind. - (2 Timothy 1:7)*

Josh had an absolute blast! He even brought back an extra pizza for me to eat - he offered slices to all of the nurses as they walked by his room. It was awesome to see his face lit up with pride. He did it. He left the hospital and got to see a glimpse of the outside world, finally!

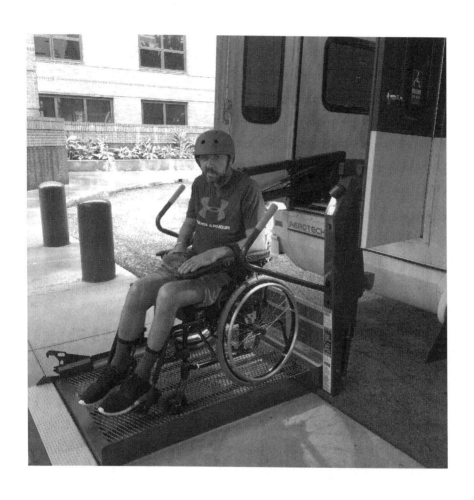

*— Josh loading the wheelchair ramp for his field trip —*

**Blog Entry - *Misled by Faith....***

I've spent most of my life telling myself that I'm in good standings with God. We had lived with a good conscious. I'm not suggesting that we haven't made our share of mistakes or that we didn't commit sin. Of course we did. We live in imperfect bodies in a cesspool of the enemy's influences with free will granted by God. Yes, we have sinned.

I saw something in Josh the first time I met him. I could feel his goodness behind the mist of what my eyes could see. Underneath his bad behavior, (as many teen boys had), his tough guy presentation and reputation that many would say symbolized "bad news" I saw a boy with a big heart. Few agreed with me at the time. In fact, even my parents forbid me to see Josh, despite knowing that I was a pretty smart girl and capable of making my own decisions.

Throughout the 20-something years I've known Josh, my judgement of him has not failed me. His heart has proven to be golden time and time again - mainly in the way he loves kids. Josh sees young people as opportunities. He wants to inspire them to make good decisions and reach beyond what he was able to do with his own youth. Having been a very talented athlete as a kid, I think Josh has major regrets about choices that he made in his teen years. I think he's lived most of his adult life wondering, "what if" as he reflects on the talents God gave him and the decisions that led him away from his passions.

For me, I have had similar thoughts - I think we all do at some point or another. But at the end of the day, I've always been content in knowing that in the present, I'm exactly where I'm supposed to be. If my past were changed, I may not be married to Josh with two incredible kids today. Reflecting on the blessings that I have, and wouldn't trade for anything in the world has always defeated any ideas of regrets.

On the subject of our faith, Josh and I have always considered ourselves children of God. We may not have appeared in church every Sunday morning, but we knew right from wrong, we prayed to God often and we lived our lives looking for ways to contribute to the good of God. We both have big hearts and great compassion for other people.
With that said, I've never seen Josh pick up a bible to read. Sadly, I've done this few times myself. We don't know the word of God, other than maybe being able to recite a few scriptures that we've heard in church.

If I'm being honest, I'm not sure if I truly even believed in the Bible - questioning the truth of words that were conveyed by man. Looking back now, I wonder if my doubts were more about justifying my faith to myself rather than seeking the truth. As human beings, I think it's our nature to try and define our weaknesses or explain them, rather than admitting to them. We don't like to feel insecure about our decisions, so we pretend we have good reason for the choices we make, even when we're in the wrong.

It was Blessing that showed me I was wrong. Well, it was GOD, but he worked through her and she was his messenger to open my eyes to the word of God. His timing couldn't have been more perfect, as only HE knew what was waiting for me in the months coming after sending Blessing to teach me. But even then, when she first approached me, I was defensive - assuring her that I was good in my faith. Again, it's uncomfortable to admit our weaknesses or bad decisions. I had been lazy in seeking God's word. I had been blind to the truth and she was sent to expose that in my own eyes.

Sometimes our biggest mistakes lie within our pride. We tell ourselves bigger lies than the ones we point out in others. If I lived every hour of every day seeking God's word, I would still be an imperfect being, needing to be closer to Him. So when I have that talk with myself - between me, myself and God, I now realize that I have to be transparent - like an open book. I can't take pride in my faith in a way that suggests, I'm good just the way I am. I have to admit that I don't know him well enough and seek him every day. I have to seek his knowledge, his word, his promises and his love for me.

Living in the light of Christ isn't a task we can complete and then be content - we will never be done with the work it takes to be close to him. It's not a final exam... It's a lifestyle of spiritual learning that only ends when our race on Earth is completed.

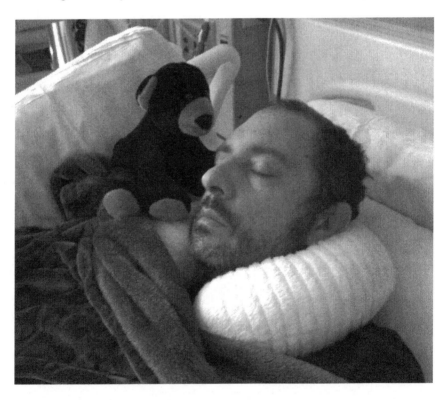

I chose the photo of Josh sleeping peacefully with his bear that was brought by a co-worker and friend – he calls it "Teddy Manfredi". I placed this photo in this post because it reminds me that placing judgement on ourselves or on others that is led by a lack of knowledge makes us ignorant. I've given Josh a hard time about this new mustache/beard look several times a day for weeks now as he refuses to let me shave his face. I laugh and kid with him, saying that he looks like a caveman or a member of Duck Dynasty.

Friday morning I asked Josh why he was so adamant about growing that awful beard out.

I said, "You don't even look like you." He said, "I look like Jesus." I asked, "that's why you won't cut your hair?" He nodded in confirmation. Needless to say, that's the last time I'll give him grief about the beard.

*"My son, pay attention to what I say; listen closely to my words. Do not let them out of your sight, keep them within your heart; for they are life to those who find them and health to a man's whole body..." (Proverbs 4:20-22)*
In Jesus' Name. Amen.

———————

Josh's sister had prepared food and deserts for a surprise *welcome home* celebration for Josh at my house. She texted me the details and asked me to keep it a surprise for Josh. His family would all be there along with my kids and our two dogs that Josh hadn't seen in nearly three months.

With plans all in place for our departure, Josh's final full day at TIRR would be a day of assessment, rather then therapy. But before that, we had our own field trip to take - back to the hospital.

TIRR coordinated a shuttle bus to pick up Josh and I from the front entrance. Two men loaded his wheelchair on the lift while I found a seat inside.

Awful memories poured into my thoughts as Josh and I made our way through long hallways to the elevator case, and finally to the nuero-science floor. This time we were in the outpatient offices for a scheduled visit with Dr. Dannenbaum.

After a 45-minute wait outside, they finally called Josh and I into a room. The nurse saw us first, asking questions and verifying information from Josh's file. Then the brain surgeon joined us and took a seat on a rolling chair, close to the ground.

He thumbed through electronic images on a large computer screen before speaking.
"I think he's ready," he announced, spinning around with a smile on his face.

The surgeon's words were music to my ears. Doctors back at TIRR warned that Josh's swelling could cause the skull replacement surgery to be delayed up to six months. I shuttered at the thought of caring for Josh at home, around kids and dogs with his skull exposed and vulnerable. Six months seemed impossible. I was ready for Josh to be back to himself now - not that the skull replacement would fix his problems, but he'd at least look somewhat human again.

"I remember you." The surgeon muttered, thumbing through data on the computer screen, once again.

"You were transferred in. Thirty-eight-year-old, sent home from the ER with a headache right before the stroke, right?"

"Yes that was him." I answered for Josh

"I'm sorry man. I wish we'd have gotten you just a little sooner." The surgeon's light blue eyes were sympathetic as he spoke to Josh.

It's hard, I guess with anything tragic, to look back and wonder what could have been different.

But now hearing the expert surgeon speak to Josh, I felt awful for my husband - thinking through the mistakes that were made by the doctors who misdiagnosed him with just a headache. I even blamed myself, wondering, *If I'd have taken him to the med center from the very beginning, would we be in this mess today?*

But, in being honest with myself, I did everything I knew to do. I took him back to the ER three times, in three consecutive days before the stroke occurred. I trusted the doctors - thinking that I lived in a world where people cared about the best interest of others - not understanding that the enemy can work through anyone, at anytime, to carry out his attacks. And at the end of the day, I should've been trusting in God instead of systems. I guess I never understood how to do that.

It was decided that Josh would have his final surgery on June 16th, the day before our 17th anniversary. The surgeon said he would spend the night in ICU, and would likely be released to go back home within a day or two.

I looked forward to getting the final surgery behind us. It would be the last medical intervention needed in my husband's brain, I hoped.

Back at TIRR, Josh started his final assessments with Speech Therapy - working through the various tests. Then moved onto

Occupational Therapy and finally arriving at Physical Therapy with Kyle.

"The purpose is to see how much he's progressed since the day he arrived here," Kyle explained, as he jotted down notes on a little scorecard after each task Josh performed.

"I want to walk out of here Kyle." Josh confessed, seeming almost irritated with the pesky assignments of the PT's final assessment.

"I know you do Josh. You're not ready, man. I'm sorry." Kyle always had spoken to Josh with sincerity. And in delivering this reality to his patient, I could see the empathy in Kyle's eyes.

"I tell you what. Let's try to walk on a walker!" Kyle clapped his hands together and sprung up from the mat, where he was seated. He re-appeared in the gym a few minutes later with a steel-bar walker that had tennis balls attached to the feet.

"You've never tried to walk without the vector. So this is going to be difficult Josh. You'll have to carry all of your weight when you stand up. So, take it easy and don't try to push yourself too hard. We're only going to take a few steps, OK?" Kyle explained, setting Josh's expectation for the trying task.

My heart was racing as Kyle and his assistant helped Josh into a standing position, and then placed his hands on top of the grips at both sides of the walker. Wanting to help, I wrapped my arm around Josh's bicep to support him in the standing position.

"OK Josh, I want you to try and take a step forward - just like you do on the vector." Kyle instructed.

Within a matter of seconds, Josh was walking - *really* walking! As Kyle shuffled at his feet, helping to keep Josh's knees in place, my husband bravely took one step after the other - turning a few steps into a journey that led into the hallway, outside of the gym.

In disbelief at what I was witnessing, I pulled out my phone and started videoing the major event. With happy tears streaming down my face I spoke out loud, "Thank you Jesus! Thank you Lord!"

---

**Facebook Post:**
He's walking without a machine for the first time today.. Down this long hall filled with stories of lives transformed by the Grace of GOD. Josh will be on this wall soon.. Inspiring others who are facing similar battles... Amen!

---

*[NOTE]: The video of Josh walking that hall at TIRR is posted on our website in the media section of www.79ministry.com.*

Josh had a hard time sleeping that night. I did too. The anticipation was eating at both of us as we had finally arrived at the day we'd been waiting for. After nearly three months, we were going home! The idea almost seemed surreal. Josh laid in bed talking about how he couldn't wait to play with our dogs and relax on the back patio by the pool. *Thank you Lord, we're going home!* I prayed to myself that night.

We spent the morning going through the motions required by TIRR before leaving to go home. Josh was taken for final scans and then once back in his room, we received a visit from a group of occupational therapists to show me how to work his permanent arm sling that he'd need to wear on his paralyzed side.

In between each appointment, I gathered another load of Josh's things and took them to my car. It was shocking how much stuff we'd accumulated in the tiny half of a hospital room we had occupied at TIRR.

"Do you want to say goodbye to anyone before we go?" I asked Josh, packing the last of his things into a small backpack as I inspected his room to make sure I hadn't left anything behind.

"Just Jeri." He loved Jeri and she loved him so much too. Jeri was his favorite nurse. No matter what floor she was working, every day Jeri made time to come by and talk with Josh. She'd been a nurse at TIRR for nearly 30 years - and shared so many stories with us about miracles she'd seen throughout her work there. Never once did Jeri brag about the facilities or the therapists - all of the success stories she shared as testimonies of God.

"You keep praying to the Good Lord above Josh. He's going to heal you. I have no doubt in my mind." She smiled and leaned down to give Josh a big hug. Jeri was always smiling. Her voice even sounded like a smile - if that were possible. She had this presence about her that was so contagious and I was thankful that she'd been part of our TIRR journey. Even on our worst days there, Jeri's visits would fill our hearts back up with hope and encouragement. She was truly an angel sent to help us through each day.

"Alright get me out of here!" Josh was ready to see his home again. I was ready too - but still dreading the car transfer to my Yukon. It was like an invisible set of arms and legs had helped me get Josh into the truck that afternoon. Unlike any of the attempts we'd made with Kyle's help, this time, we did it almost effortlessly. Josh even found the strength to stand without me having to dead-lift the impossible weight that my body couldn't bear. God lifted him into that truck on angels wings.

The enemy tried to convince me that God had let me down that day. I had claimed that Josh would walk out of TIRR - I'd prayed and I'd confessed and I'd believed. Josh didn't walk out of TIRR. But God did deliver in his own way. Although the Lord hadn't answered my prayers the way I thought they should've been answered - he did show up. He gave us the miracle of Josh walking down the hall for the first time on a walker. And he gave us the miracle of providing me the strength to load Josh into the car for the very first time without assistance. *God is good.*

But before I could even finish celebrating the help of God that had lifted Josh into my truck, another storm was on the way. Literally, the roads became so dangerous, I couldn't see but a few feet in front of my windshield. It was raining so heavily, vehicles with hazards blinking were pulling to the shoulder of the freeway.

I prayed silently for the rain to subside. "Please Lord calm the storm and help me get Josh home safely." I knew he couldn't take a car accident even of a small magnitude. A jolt to his exposed brain could be fatal.

"Why are you driving so fast?" Josh asked. His voice was panicky and winded.

"Baby, I'm barely going 30 and the speed limit is 60," I explained.

"I'm dizzy. I'm about to throw up." Josh's face was pale and his cheeks were flushed with hints of pink.

*Is he getting carsick or is something else happening to Josh?*, I wondered. *Why did no one warn me that he would have trouble traveling in a car?* My anxiety was stirring as I thought about turning back to the hospital. We were still more than a half-hour drive to our home, and I was scared that if something went wrong with Josh, I'd not be able to get him back to the hospital through the torrential rain.

I thumbed around in the backseat to find a large cup, in case Josh were to start vomiting. Then I started conversation with Josh about home. I told him how happy the dogs would be to see him and reminded him of how wonderful it would be to relax in the comfort of his own couch - watching football on the big screen. As my mouth went in one direction, my thoughts were somewhere completely different - I was in silent prayer, asking God to get us home safely. And as soon as we crossed over 610, blue skies appeared up ahead. The rain stopped and I knew He'd heard me. *Thank you Lord.*

We had a houseful waiting on Josh to arrive at our home. When we pulled up, Josh's dad came out to greet us. He helped me get Josh from the truck to his wheelchair and excitedly pointed out to Josh the custom ramps he'd built at the doorway, so Josh's wheelchair could get in and out of our exits.

Josh's sister Tiffany was there with her husband and their son. His brother had his two kids, his girlfriend, and her daughter with them. And Josh's mom was there too. Our children MaeKenna and Lil Josh were like tour guides for their dad - one walking on each side of his wheelchair pointing out to him all the food his family had brought over and calling the dogs. "Look Bentley! Daddy's home! Boomer come say hi to Daddy!"

After we ate pasta and salad, Vivian and Tiffany helped me clean up the kitchen, while Josh sat in the living room visiting with his dad and Van. I heard MaeKenna's piano playing from the front room. "Jodi?" Josh looked around searching the room for me. His vision remained limited, according to the doctors at TIRR. Due to the left neglect condition, Josh had no peripheral view and could only see things that were positioned to his right side.

"What ya need babe?" I threw the hand towel down and made my way to the living room. "I want to hear Maekenna play." I wheeled Josh down the hallway into the study where MaeKenna was singing the song she had written for her dad.

*"Oh-oh Father, it's not your time, and our father is by your side and he's healing... you're shattered wounds, cause Jesus.. died for you.."*

As she sang the song he'd only before heard over a video chat conversation from within the hospital, Josh fell to pieces before me -

sobbing and shaking. I wiped a tear drop from his cheek. "Baby are you ok? What's wrong?" He buried his face inside of his t-shirt and sobbed even harder.

"Why are you sad, Josh?" I asked, trying to search his expression to figure out if he was crying tears of sadness or happiness.

"I just.. I was scared I'd never see this place again." He struggled to get out the words as tears overflowed from his eyes. I dropped to my knees beside his wheelchair and placed my head against his. We cried together for at least 10 minutes while MaeKenna sang a variety of songs about Jesus.

"Josh come back in here and spend time with your family." Vivian appeared with a big smile and a chirpy voice. "I'm tired." He whispered, quickly wiping the tears from his face. "I'm sorry son. I'll tell everyone to leave so you can get some rest."

I didn't quite understand why Josh seemed so distant from his family during their welcome home dinner. Later, he would tell me how scared he had felt on that day. He explained that it seemed like he was stuck in a dark tunnel - hearing voices around him but not being able to find anyone. I can't imagine what that must have been like for him - the confusion with  sounds of kids playing and multiple conversations happening at once. The extent of Josh's brain damage wasn't fully understood to us. And doctors told me that every injury to the brain was different. They just weren't sure what all had been lost or what Josh may have suffered - deficits that would only become more evident after we were home.

Our first night at home was stressful for me. I sifted through instructions that TIRR had printed - organizing all of his prescriptions and preparing a meal plan for breakfast the next day.

Then, we attempted the shower for the first time without assistance. It was tough. No - tough isn't the right word. It was impossible! Yet, no one got hurt. I wrestled with Josh's body, nervous that I would drop him as we transferred from the wheelchair into the rolling shower harness.

Miraculously, we made it through the first night of challenges. At last, Josh was comfortable in the little hospital bed that was installed in the corner of our master bedroom. He seemed peaceful, thumbing through the channels on our big screen TV. It was an amazing feeling to finally have my husband and my children all sleeping underneath the same roof again. We were *finally* home.

# Chapter Nine

# *It is* Finished

## He is Faithful

Josh spent most of his time sleeping after we arrived back home. When he was awake, he stared into space. He hardly spoke - giving only short answers when I asked him questions. Josh was there with me, but *not there with me*, it seemed. I missed him terribly. And as much I hated to admit it, depression was settling into my thoughts almost hourly.

Home life now, was nothing like it had been before Josh had left in an ambulance on that horrible night in March. Tremendous loss was evident in every passing moment. Josh's presence was like that of an infant in many ways. He was there with us and we could talk to him and love on him through the days and nights that passed. But his participation in our lives as a father and husband was missing. He seemed almost unaware of his surroundings - locked into deep thoughts in a secret world that I couldn't begin to understand.

"What are you thinking about?" I asked him repeatedly in attempt to break through the trance-like state that he lived in as he sat in his wheelchair staring into space throughout most of each day.

"Nothing." He would answer every time I asked.

Assuming that depression had taken hold of him too, I tried my best to keep Josh stimulated with board games and activities. But the more I tried, the more Josh's disabilities were brought to the surface.

"Dad, you're supposed to put the blue dots in a row." Josh Jr. explained to his father as they attempted to play a game of *Connect-4*.

"I already have four." Josh argued with our son, confused and frustrated that he wasn't able to count that high.

Tasks that were easy to small children, were impossible now for Josh. And I wondered how we'd ever find our way back to a normal life again.

My broken heart played through years of memories inside of my tears, revealing a great sense of regret. I thought about how much I had taken for granted in the years that had passed us by - wishing I'd held Josh a little closer, walked a little slower and lived a more meaningful marriage by his side.

The surgery to replace Josh's skull couldn't come quick enough. The hospital had kept his skull piece in a freezer over the last several months awaiting the swelling in Josh's brain to subside. I was looking forward to the procedure. Getting it behind us would mean no more surgeries, hopefully. And, I'd read research implying that some patients showed great progress after their skulls were put back together. It had something to do with the brain's ability to pressurize. I didn't understand all the scientific articles I'd read, I only knew that it was another milestone that could give us new hope. And I needed new hope badly.

Watching my husband day in and day out, almost zombie-like with no personality and no communication skills was depressing, at best. Plus, the physical strain on me was exhausting. Josh couldn't do anything by himself. I had to dress him, bathe him, feed him, change his diapers and load him on and off of the hospital bed we'd had installed in our bedroom, repeatedly throughout each day. On top of all that, I was still trying to at least do some real estate business to keep income for the family and trying to find time to raise two kids. I need a break-through and I needed it fast.

**Blog Entry - *Home...***

There are moments when I feel normalcy settling in my mood. It's great to be home, where we are a family brought back together – all sleeping under the same roof at night. Then there are moments when sadness creeps up. The reality of how limited we are in simple things like checking the mail or doing a load of laundry.

I fear leaving Josh for even a few minutes. He's overly confident of what he can do, and that scares me. Already he's tried to transfer himself twice – once to the couch in the living room and once to the bed set-up in our master. His last doctor said that a false understanding of what he's capable of is part of the stroke. He said Josh may believe that he can do things not yet possible, physically. I think it's more of Josh's will to get better. Josh told me last night, "It's so hard after 39 years to not be able to just get up and walk to the bathroom." Feeling the loss of function isn't something he's not aware of – he's very aware; and that is why he tries so hard to overcome it.

I wrote last night about strength only found in God. I see this test challenging Josh more than any of us. Josh's physical strength was one of his biggest assets. He was so strong, so fast, so athletic and so able to do just about any task he put his mind to. I remember once watching him move furniture with our hired crew. There were 4 men on one side of the piece and only Josh on the other. I swear he had more power than the other 4 combined. I can't imagine how he feels with that taken away from him – just like that – in the blink of an eye... gone.

Home is calming and therapeutic. He loves his family and really enjoys playing with his dogs. But home is also awakening, I'm sure. He sees his things, his stairway to his theater that he had spent so much time building, his swimming pool sparkling on a hot day and he can't enjoy any of these things. I told him, "Soon, you'll be in there swimming again." He responded with, "we hope."

Hebrews 11:1 says - "Now faith is the substance of things hoped for, the evidence of things not seen." I do hope Josh will be swimming and enjoying his pool very soon. But more than hope - I have FAITH.

I have faith that every knee will bow at the powerful name of Jesus Christ, who's stripes paid the highest price of Josh's healing. I have faith that God's word is above everything in and out of existence and his promises will reveal newness in Josh's body - HE will make Josh whole again.

Tomorrow we start outpatient therapy in the Woodlands. We have to leave at 6:30 in the morning and then continue the rest of the week on this new schedule. Then on Thursday of next week, Josh has to be at the Nueroscience ICU again for his final surgery. The next two weeks will bring much change and many new challenges as well. I will continue to give all of my trust to God and I know in my heart that Josh will be healed completely in the coming weeks.

Still in the storm but I see the light ahead.......

———————————

Prior to leaving TIRR, the social worker set us up to continue therapy at their Woodlands location - three times a week for three hours each day. But due to an administrative error in the system at TIRR, we woke up at the crack of dawn and drove nearly an hour away to our first day of outpatient therapy for no reason. They didn't have Josh scheduled with any therapists yet. And our newly assigned case worker explained that the doctors had decided to delay Josh's schedule, due to his upcoming surgery.

She said that the surgery could change Josh's prognosis for the good or the bad. And change would require the assessment process to start all over again.

I was bummed. I missed that daily struggle to get better that we had known inside of TIRR. I missed the support of therapists, like cheerleaders encouraging Josh to try new things. I missed activity - the feeling that we were doing something productive in taking steps toward Josh's recovery. Home life was like time wasting away in my carnal thoughts. Home was a lingering feeling of loneliness in my pursuit to walk with Josh through recovery and towards a new chapter that I continued to beg the Lord to reveal before us.

--------

**Blog Entry - *Hebrews 10:35***
My mother sent me this scripture today, the perfect words at the perfect time....

"So do not throw away your confidence; it will be richly rewarded. You need to persevere so that when you have done the will of God, you will receive what he has promised." - *(Hebrews 10:35)*

Prior to receiving this message, I broke down into tears when Rex, Josh's roommate from TIRR, sent a video clip of him walking with the assistance of his therapists today.

217

The text message came as a message from God – a wake-up call in the midst of my despair.

Coming home has been bitter-sweet for me. I'm happy because we're finally in our own home with our kids and our pets – a much more comfortable environment than the hospital room. But coming home also is challenging.

I have no nurses or doctors to consult with if Josh's swelling is up or any symptoms surface – like today, his swelling appeared to be increasing. It's also very exhausting. Josh is literally twice my size and transferring from the bed to the chair to the shower is quickly taking a toll on my body. I can handle the pain, I just worry that I will pull something one of these times, which would be awful if I were to become limited because he needs me to take care of him.

Overwhelmed by so many things running through my head today – the surgery next week, the appearance of new swelling, the struggle I feel physically, I started feeling very emotional. It was, as I said, perfect timing to get the text message from Rex.

We aren't in therapy for two weeks because of the scheduled surgery but that doesn't mean that Josh is not progressing and will not pick right up where we left off. I felt myself today reaching out to God – straining for his comfort.

Tonight, I realize where I'm going wrong. I was once again allowing myself to worry. I was stressing over decisions regarding Josh, over his swelling, over things I need to do around the house, over work related items I have to attend to and it all seemed so overwhelming.

God told me to give this to him when we started this journey. He assured me that everything would be alright, but it was required that I trust him completely. I think when I start worrying, it's as if I'm trying to pull the responsibility back on myself and I have to take a step back and give it back to God again - I have to regroup and assure God that I don't want this worry and I don't want to try to find the answers, but instead I want to trust HIM for the answers.

*Tonight, God, I lift Josh up and lay him at the feet of Jesus. I request Father a healing of Josh's physical body here on Earth - I ask you to free Josh from the physical sickness that attacked him and complete the miracle that you have started. I ask you to heal our hearts Father. Jesus, as you've paid the highest price, Josh is set free tonight. Jesus, Josh's body will heal only in your name as you are the one who sacrificed for his healing - by the stripes on your flesh, Josh is healed. Jesus, I rest my worries and Josh's health at the foot of your cross and ask you to bless us with a complete miracle. Father I know that Josh was left here on Earth for a reason - he was renewed and made a testimony of your glory.*

*I know that his story will bring glory to your name and I thank you Father for the blessings we are receiving. Tonight, I declare his healing by the blood of Christ, I declare his swelling gone, I declare his brain healed, I declare his body renewed and every cell, every nerve, every organ renewed to perfect health by the power of the Holy Spirit and the name of JESUS CHRIST!*
*In Jesus' Name... Amen.*

---

Surprising news sent shock into our morning, when Bridget, (Adam's wife) called me from TIRR to ask how we were doing. In conversation she asked, "You knew that Jeri passed away, right?" According to

Bridget, Josh's favorite nurse had passed away from a heart attack the day after we were sent home from TIRR.

I could hardly grasp the peculiar news. Jeri Brooks was an important part of our journey - the happy, cheerful woman that stopped by Josh's hospital room several times a day to brighten our moods.

---

### Blog Entry - *RIP Jeri Brooks - Our Angel*

There was a nurse at TIRR that was unlike anyone else that cared for Josh. She had something very special about her, very pure and up-lifting. She loved Josh. I could see it in her eyes. Even on the days when she wasn't assigned to him, she'd stop by at least once to check on him. She raved about how great he is doing and left words of encouragement. Her voice was raspy, yet full of cheer.

A few weeks back we talked to Jeri about Nate Lytle, the author of "More God," a book that Josh and I were reading nightly together. Jeri had cared for Nate when he was at TIRR. She shared stories about him - how bad it was and how amazing his miraculous recovery was. Jeri took my hand and said, "Josh is going to heal completely too." I couldn't help but burst out into tears at the sincerity in her gesture. She said, "I have no doubt in my mind. I can tell the ones who are going to make it." Days after she would stop in randomly to tell us about other patients who had received the miracle of God.

Two days before Josh was discharged, Jeri left a note on his bed. She said that she had something for him and she's sorry she missed us but would come back later. That night I ran into her at the bottom of the elevator case as she was leaving for home. She was beaming with pride as she explained that she was going to be a grandma and it was time for the baby to

220

come. I hugged her to wish her well on her way home and she said, "No, come here, I have something - it's not much but I couldn't stop thinking about Josh last night." She pulled from her bag a piece of tissue paper that read "Iron Bill" and then a silver frame with a printed story inside of it and lastly a sticker of a brain image with a heart inside of it.

She explained that she'd woke up in the middle of the night to write on that piece of paper to tell Josh about Iron Bill's story. She rambled about how I needed to research his amazing story and share it with Josh. Then, she pointed out the image of the brain with the heart and said "This was his actual catscan." It appeared the entire brain was damaged, except for the perfect shape of a heart in the center of the brain. "Wow!" I couldn't hardly find the words as Jeri's eyes filled with tears and she continued to explain that the man healed completely. "I kept this sticker for so long. I want Josh to have it." Jerry offered, handing me a sticker with the heart catscan on it. "I thought he could wear it on his helmet." Jeri hugged my neck and cried with me happy tears, as if to say to me that we will be one of those stories of miracles that she so optimistically shared with me.

I missed Jeri on Wednesday as we prepared for discharge from TIRR but was very excited for her to welcome her first grand baby into the world. Then on Thursday, Jeri's smiling face ran into our room first thing in the morning. She was shaking her cell phone in the air as she showed off the picture of the beautiful little newborn. I felt so happy for her - she was just on cloud nine. "I haven't seen her yet." She told us. Apparently they didn't take the baby until Thursday morning so Jeri's day off awaiting the baby on Wednesday didn't work out with God's schedule for the little girl to enter our world.

Thursday night Jeri ended her shift by visiting Josh's room as she often did. She came in to say goodbye and to tell Josh how great he was doing, as usual. Josh told her to go see her grandbaby and Jeri said she wasn't sure that she would make it that evening because the weather was so bad. Josh said, "Just drive slow. But go see her, it's worth it." Jeri pondered his words and then smiled her normal big smile. She hugged Josh and then hugged me and said, "I've got goose bumps again." She often said she had goose bumps when she looked at Josh. Her eyes would water over and she would say how great he's doing and remind Josh that she is certain he will recover completely. On this night she said, "You're going to heal because you have this angel next to you," signaling to me.

That was the last time we saw Jeri. Although Friday morning, when I asked Josh if he wanted to say goodbye to any of the nurses before we left, he only mentioned her name.

Jeri passed away on Monday. I got the news from Adam's wife on Tuesday night. My heart breaks for her family - her children. But I feel so blessed to have known her and for all the encouragement and love she provided to Josh during his stay at TIRR. Jeri was the one nurse on this journey that I will never forget.

I can't help but wondering if God's plan for Jeri included Josh - if maybe HE kept Jeri here to see Josh through the end of his stay at TIRR. I just can't explain the love in her eyes and the sincere care that she felt for Josh. She treated him like he was a miracle - like she couldn't see that he was not yet healed completely. She treated us both with such love and her presence always brightened our mood.

Jeri, I love you and I am so thankful that Josh and I were blessed with the opportunity to know you. RIP Angel…

*Dear God, thank you for sending us this angel, Jeri Brooks. God, please comfort her family and provide them all with peace. I know Jeri is with you in Heaven tonight, where you need her. God I thank you for lending her to Josh and I before taking your angel to your Kingdom. We will never forget her and the inspiration she provided to us both.*

*In Jesus' Name, Amen.*

---

Jeri's departure into her forever home in Heaven was shocking and sad, yet in a strange way, revealing another purple stone in our lives. I wondered if God had kept her here the perfect number of days to see Josh through his stay at TIRR. It was odd that she passed the day after we went home. And, there was no doubt in my mind that she had been given to us as an angel to encourage us through a difficult time.

As the days ticked away, closer to surgery time, a cloud of nervousness settled in over our household. The familiar presence of anxiety and worry, led me to the place where I knew strength came from - prayer and meditation on God. I searched for images of good news in our future and battled to place aside my temporary troubles to believe in a plan that would work out of our good.

*And we know that all things work together for good to them that love God, to them who are the called according to his purpose. - (Romans 8:28, NIV)*

---

**Blog Entry - *2 More Days..***
My emotions are as predictable as the weather right now. In one moment I feel excited and optimistic and in the next I'm nervous

223

about the unknown in our recent future. Here's what I do know - God showed me a completely healed Josh. When I clung to His word and refused to believe the reports of the doctors and that of my own eyes, HE showed me HIS plan for Josh. I am blessed by this promise and keep it close to my heart as we prepare for our last human intervention into Josh's brain this coming Thursday.

We are three days away from surgery - expected to arrive at Hermann Neuroscience ICU at 6:30a.m. on Thursday morning. The procedure is called a Cranioplasty, consisting of replacing the skull piece, or bone flap as the doctors refer to it. It will only leave Josh in the hospital for a day or two.

On March 26, a large piece of Josh's skull covering the entire right side of his head was removed and placed in a freezer at Hermann. Another surgery took place just hours after this initial procedure to remove tissue from Josh's brain and a portion of muscle that runs between Josh's ear and right eye. Following the surgeries Josh's brain was able to swell out, relieving pressure off of Josh's brain stem and also correcting the mid-line shift in Josh's brain. A mid-line shift greater than 10mm is usually fatal. I don't know the exact numbers of Josh's - I was only told he had a "severe" mid-line shift. I also don't yet have any details on the bleeding or swelling that prompted the second surgery, but I did read in a study that the immediate revision presents 5% to 10% survival rate.

Oh how our God has surpassed statistics while holding Josh in his hands.

How can I be worried when I'm faced with facts of how far we've come? God did this. God defied all odds - HE defied science and HE is working a miracle in Josh. This surgery is I believe a milestone in our journey. Josh will be put back together and with all of his body parts once again in tact, God will finish what HE has started.

I've spent a lot of time the last two days doing the thing I try not to do - researching on the internet. Normally these research sessions don't bring good news. When I've read about Josh's injury in the past, I've been faced with horrid statistics. But researching this, I find information supporting my hope and my FAITH. In one study, every single patient regained the ability to walk following cranioplasty. In other studies, the majority of patients saw increase function in limb movement, memory, speech and a number of other areas that had been effected by brain injury.

Some studies imply the docs "don't know" why improvements are seen following replacement of the skull. But others studies provide insight on data and images and tests indicating improvements involving pressurizing of the brain and cerebral fluid. One article even discussed how the missing skull piece can negatively effect the non-injured side of the brain due to the issues with fluid distribution and improperly balanced pressure.

*What does all of this mean?*
To me it means, get ready for the revealing of another blessing. I know God has renewed and repaired damage that was done to Josh's brain. I've seen the process and the proof of his work! This Thursday when Josh's pieces are placed back together as God had created him, I believe we will see just how much God has completed in Josh. I believe Josh will be completely restored very, very soon.

*Keep us in your prayers as Josh goes in for his final brain surgery. I can't wait to tell everyone about God's amazing grace when this procedure is behind us. Josh is in God's Hands!*

## Blog Entry - Going Back ....

We got the call this afternoon. Josh will be taken in at 10:30 for preparation and they plan to operate at 12:30 tomorrow.

In this passage I want to speak to God. So many things weigh on my chest - much like the way I felt the first time I walked into our home after Josh had left in the ambulance that night. I'm not afraid of this surgery - God I know that you have him in your hands. I know your promise and I know your word is above all. I know you will protect him and deliver him back to me and the kids in perfect health. Father, still I ask you to give me strength. I ask you to give me confidence so strong that nothing can shake me to fear. Father when I see those tiled green floors that lead down the long hallway - Father when I hear the machines and the helicopters and the medical teams rushing into those rooms, let me feel only your peace.

I don't want to forget where we have been. I know this trial has made us stronger, wiser in you and has changed our lives so drastically that we will never be the same. I also don't want to go back. I never again want to feel that hopelessness as I watched Josh fighting for his life. I ask you God to complete this miracle. I believe you God that the worst is over and that Josh will be renewed and made whole again - I believe that we are knocking on the door - so close to the beauty of your grand finale. Let me rest in your truth God. Let me fill my heart with your love. Let me boast in your grace as the glory belongs all to you, my Lord.

I believe this final intervention that puts Josh's body back in tact that way that God created it will be a major milestone in his full recovery. I believe his peripheral vision will be back 100%. I believe his mind, his arms, his legs and every function intended by his perfect body will made perfect once again. I believe my

Father in Heaven will reveal his plan to renew Josh and I believe my husband will come home no longer needing a wheelchair, or an arm brace. I believe HE IS HEALED.

Thank you God for this miracle I am watching before my eyes. I can not wait to see your finished blessing.

In Jesus Name. Amen.

---

We arrived an hour before the scheduled surgery, as instructed. My mother showed up with the kids to offer support. Josh was nervous - his dark brown eyes almost appeared to be shaking as he talked to the nurses that started his IV. They placed a heated blanket over him to keep him warm while we waited for his doctor.

About 15 minutes after the hour, a male nurse appeared to give us an update. "We just got a young kid in with a massive TBI. Your surgeon has been pulled away to operate on him. We're going to be delayed." He explained.

"Do you know how long?" I asked the young nurse.

"Uhhh.. it's pretty serious. The kid jumped out of a car moving 90 miles per hour. It could be 2 hours or it could be 10 depending on how extensive the damage is."

My mood changed instantly from feeling sorry for Josh that he'd have to sit here anxiously to feeling awful for that young man and his family. I remembered all too well the night Josh was pulled into 2 emergency brain surgeries - the hopelessness and the fear in wondering whether he'd survive the operating table.

"That's awful. Thank you for the update." I said, excusing the nurse.

About 3 hours had passed when the young man appeared again. "They're just about ready for Josh." He announced, pulling a tray of medical materials behind him. "Only one person is allowed to go back

227

with Josh as we prep him for surgery." I stepped forward, handing my mother all of my belongings. I knew the drill - I'd not be allowed to bring anything that wouldn't fit in my pockets with me.

When I made it to to the recovery room / preparation room, Josh was surrounded by a team of medical staff. A younger guy told him jokes and kept him entertained as they worked on him. "What kind of cocktail you like Josh? Tequila? Rum?" He was preparing the anesthesia to put Josh under. I grabbed Josh's right hand and kissed him on the cheek.

"You want a full shave or just the side we're operating on?" A shorter man asked, wearing a set of blue scrubs. "Just shave what you need to." Josh answered, moving his neck to the side to try and find the man's face.

"Baby everything's going to be fine. God is with us." I whispered into Josh's ear. "I hope so." He replied as a small pool of moisture puddled into his eyes.

"Miss Manfred, it's time. We'll bring him back to you in a few hours." The short blonde nurse signaled with his arm that I had to leave.

It was a long day already with the early morning commute and the unexpected several-hour delay to begin Josh's surgery. I met up with my mom and the kids downstairs to eat a late lunch in the hospital cafeteria. The kids were starving. But I couldn't even look at food much less attempt to put anything in my nervous stomach.

I sat at the table doing my best act of pretending to be calm - but my mind was fixated on that knife opening Josh's brain again. I needed to be alone. I needed to pray.

I asked my mom to stay with the kids then I quickly walked the long hallway and down two staircases to the front entrance. Fresh air and the big blue sky always had helped me to feel God's presence when we were living in the hospital.

Once outside I found a small patch of grass to the side of the building, dropped to my knees and released a wave of tears that had been waiting to escape since we'd arrived that morning. I tried to be strong for Josh and for the kids - smiling and encouraging everyone that this surgery would go well. But inside I felt like I was hanging off the side of a cliff by a string - desperately grasping at God's promises in hopes of the outcome I desired.

"Father, please send your angels to that operating table right now! God, please bring him through this procedure without any complications. I can't take anymore. God please hear me. I can't take anymore complications or problems or hospital stays. Please Father....."

I cried into the palm of my hands, sitting alone on that lawn. As I let it all come out of me - weeping and shaking violently, I heard two words that struck me down so powerfully and suddenly that I immediately fell into complete stillness and silence - *"It's over."*

*It's over? Is that you God? What do you mean it's over?*

I'd never heard the Holy Spirit speak to me before Josh's stroke. I didn't even know if I believed in such a thing. But I know now - that feeling that can't be explained when a message comes from a source that I know isn't me (not my thoughts) and immediately causes drastic change in my thoughts and my body's behavior. Once again, I felt the peace of Jesus, and that waterfall of grace over me. My crying was stopped and my fear was gone instantly. If I were searching for meaning in that message, "It's over" using *my* logic, I would probably have been a wreck. *Over* means *ending*, right? It's over could've meant that Josh had just stopped breathing right there on the operating table. But through the perfect peace of the answer I desired during prayer to the Lord, I was given understanding that our days of hospitals, surgeries and medical intervention were over. God told me that the worst was behind us. He told me that my prayer would be answered and Josh would come out of that surgery with flying colors and we'd never be back to Nuero-ICU again, after that day. *He said... IT'S OVER.*

*John 10:30 - My sheep hear my voice, and I know them, and they follow me:*

I was so excited about the message from the Lord, I wanted to tell someone. So, I decided to tell Josh - not directly. But I wrote him a letter with my own internal interpretation of God's message and what it would mean for our future. Here is the letter I wrote to Josh while in the waiting room outside of his brain surgery that was taking place:

*Dear Josh,*

*You're in surgery right now having your skull replaced. It's been about an hour since they wheeled you away and the docs said you should be out in an hour to an hour and a half. I close my eyes and see the grace of God working on your brain. I see the power of Jesus working in every hand that's laid on you right now. On the 3rd day, God rose Jesus from the dead. And in your 3rd surgery, in the third month since you're injury, God is raising you from this sickness. Josh, today I believe in our future together. I believe you are healed by our Father in Heaven. I love you so much! God gave me you when I was just a kid and I know he's giving you back to me again healed. Together we will love deeper, we will glorify God with our lives and we will be happier than ever before. Today, we are freed of our sins and you are free of this sickness because Jesus bared your sickness on a tree. Today is the first day of the rest of our lives. Your lucky 17 is tomorrow. And for our 17 year anniversary on June 17, we will start new. Jesus made us new inside and out by the power of our Heavenly Father. By his stripes we are healed!*

*As we wait for our surgeon to report that your surgery is completed and is a success, my heart is filled with faith in God & faith in you. I know you are leaning on him with everything you have, for your strength. And I admire how much you've grown spiritually. Both of our souls are now saved and we are bound together by our Father in Heaven. I love you so much. I love how beautiful your heart is. I love how much you love me. I love how much you love our children. I love how wonderful our lives will soon be together. All the love we have will prosper into God's beautiful miracle he has for you. This is our new beginning baby! This is the end of the storm! Jesus was in the boat with us the whole time and he did not fail us! He defeated the enemy! We made it to the other side. God is lifting us up with his righteous right hand. Joy is ours by the perfect name of Jesus Christ.*

*Love,*
*Your soulmate for life & beyond in Heaven*
*after we fulfill God's plan for us here. - Jodi*


The surgery was anticipated to take only an hour. So at the three hour mark, I was becoming nervous. I paced back and forth in the crowded waiting room. I walked the hall to the restroom to splash cold water on my face a few times. I repeated to myself over and over again "It is done. By the stripes of Jesus it is finished."

Finally, I spotted Josh's surgeon walking through a set of large double doors. He immediately smiled when he saw my face and instant relief fell upon me.

"It's all done. He did well - it took longer than we thought because he had two skull flaps from the separate surgeries. I had to connect those two pieces together before I could screw everything in place."

Dr. Dannenbaum had originally told me that Josh would have to spend the night in ICU. I had been a little nervous about this, considering we had so many traumatic memories of living on that floor. But, the surgeon delivered music to my ears, "Josh is in recovery now and then I'm having him sent to a regular room. I didn't have to expose his brain so there's no need for Josh to stay the night in ICU." I thanked the doctor and gave him a big hug. Then I excused myself from the family to find a quiet corner where I could drop to my knees and thank the Lord for delivering Josh out of his final brain surgery. *He is faithful.*

The hour in recovery turned into late hours of the night and I just couldn't take it anymore. I asked the nurse and the waiting room station

231

why Josh hadn't been moved to a room yet. She was quick to inform me that there were no rooms. "We're still waiting on somewhere to send him Miss Manfred. A room hasn't opened up yet."

I guess she saw the anxiety written on my face because a few minutes later, she approached me. "Can you come with me?" The lady explained that no visitors were allowed in recovery. But they were willing to make an exception because Josh had been screaming for me non-stop. Visions of him screaming my name were troubling and as I followed the woman through a maze of hallways and doorways blocked by name-tag security clearance entries, I worried about him. *Was he scared? Was he in pain? Why was he **screaming** for me?*

I wasn't prepared for what I would see in recovery - Josh's head down to his chest was covered in blood. As soon as he spotted me, his face crinkled up like a little boy that had just dropped his lollipop - he started balling - crying. "Oh baby, what is it?" I studied Josh, calculating his wounds to see where all the blood was coming from, assuming his tears were due to excruciating pain.

"Are you hurting? What's wrong baby?" After several minutes passed, Josh finally caught his breath in the midst of weeping. He looked up at me with the most pitiful eyes I'd ever seen and muttered, "I lived."

Tears of joy took over me. "Yes baby, God did it. You lived!"

*Faithful is he that calleth you, who also will do it. - (Thessalonians 5:24)*

## — *It's over* —

It was almost midnight before we were transferred from recovery to a hospital room. It was quiet. Josh was given pain medicine and he slept heavily through the night. Around 8 in the morning a female doctor came in to check on Josh. She wrote in her clipboard and advised that a nurse would be in soon with release paperwork for Josh to go home. We were told prior to coming in that Josh would have to stay in the hospital at least 3 days following the procedure.

"Are you sure he's ready to go home? He just had surgery last night."

"His stitches look good. The scans came back fine. We're releasing him this morning."

Talking with doctors is hit or miss. They either tell me way too much information on subjects that I'd rather not discuss - like complications and worst case scenarios, or they hardly say anything and make me wonder if they're functioning on partial facts.

The drive home was optimistic. Josh was still feeling the effects of heavy doses of pain medicine and seemed in good spirits. I stopped to get him a subway sandwich from Lenny's and then once home, I helped him to his hospital bed. Jim had a crew working on our hardwood floors while we were away, so the bed had been moved to the living room. Josh didn't mind. He went straight to sleep.

---

## Blog Entry - God Released His Angels

We are home. Expecting to stay in the hospital a couple days, I'm full of thanks to our Almighty God that Josh's stay at MH was cut short. His surgery went very well and last night the catscan results by his surgeon's words were "perfect", prompting an immediate discharge this morning.

Last night Josh complained of severe head pain but by this morning the pain had subsided a great amount. He has mild swelling on the right side of his head and above his ear, but that too will be gone soon as I know this event was completely and utterly controlled by our Father. Driving home this afternoon Josh said, "I know Jesus was with me yesterday." I asked, "How do you know?" Josh explained, "I was really nervous and then I started praying and suddenly I wasn't nervous anymore. I was completely calm and I knew then he was with me."

I got a chance to take a second look at the Jones Pavilion Neuroscience Unit. For example, the weary green tiled hallway that seemed to never end wasn't quite as dark this go round. I noticed things like artistic paintings on the wall and smiles on the faces of bystanders - things that seemed to be missing from my last stay. We spent over 4 weeks in that hospital in the beginning of this journey. There were days I worried my heart would jump right out of my chest or I'd just drop to the floor and stop breathing all together. That nightmare is over. God has pulled us from the wreckage and claimed our lives under his will that we will prosper and be in good health.

After the surgeon came to speak with us yesterday to share the good news that it was over and all had went well, I took a few minutes to myself to go outside and just stare at the sky and the trees. It was a gorgeous day, the opposite of what we'd seen in the weeks leading up to here of thunderstorms and tireless rain. I felt a calm that came over me too - like Josh had explained. For me, the voice inside said, "It's over." And I knew that from this day forward we are climbing uphill only. No more sickness. No more setbacks. No more attacks from the enemy. God has us in his hands and he will continue to lift us up each day forward.

Josh - Happy Anniversary Sweetheart... Today is the first day of the rest of our lives with Jesus at our side. I can't wait to see the beauty he has in store for us.

———————————

Josh slept for the next 24 hours, waking briefly to eat and take his medicines, then went back to sleep again. Everything seemed to be going fine until day 2 post surgery. Josh's face began swelling at a rapid pace to the point that his eye was completely shut. As we headed into the night, the swelling had traveled all the way down to his neck. His head looked like a basketball and I was worried that the swelling may impact his ability to breath.

I checked on him periodically and tried to wake him just to make sure he was still breathing and speaking. He was groggy, but did his best to participate in my drills. "Josh can you hear me?" "hmm," he mumbled. "Babe are you breathing ok?" "mhmmm."

Around midnight I tried to wake him to adjust his pillows - remembering the nurses instructions to keep his head elevated. When I lifted up the back of his shoulders, the pillow moved with his head. It was stuck. I turned on a light to see if the stitches were causing an issue to discover a huge puddle of blood running from the top of Josh's head to his now soaked crimson stained pillow.

I quickly dialed the emergency line that was provided in Josh's release paperwork - reading through the warnings as I was placed on hold. It said that if I spotted any blood from the wound, to call immediately.

The nurse took my information and said she would attempt to reach Josh's surgeon. But as the seconds passed like hours, worry creeped into my thoughts.

I went into panic mode, packing a bag and throwing a pair of jeans on. "Josh I have to take you to the hospital. Wake up Josh!" I shouted, flipping on the lights and searching the pile of clothes on the floor for Josh's shoes. He didn't respond - he was out cold, in a deep sleep.

I decided I'd load the car and have everything ready to go before I woke him. But as I worked quickly to pull myself together and throw my long, ratted hair into a pony tail in front of our master bedroom vanity, I lost my strength. It's like the room was caving in on me and dizziness took my breath away.

"God you said it was over. You told me it was over! Where are you God? Are you even here? Do you even care what's happening?"

I fell to my knees and tried to cry out to the Lord in prayer for help. I needed strength but had none. As the room spun around me faster and faster I grew more anxious, realizing that I was in no condition to make the hour drive to the med center. The anxiety attack threw me back to that night when Josh had collapsed in our living room. I couldn't handle another emergency. Didn't God know I wasn't strong enough for this? Realizing my only option to take Josh back in, was to call 911 and have an ambulance transport Josh, I crawled to my purse and sifted through the mess of papers and receipts searching for my cell phone. It wasn't there. *Great! I lost my phone and I can't stop spinning to get up and look for it.*

In sobbing tears I fell from my knees to my stomach, flat faced on the cold tile floor in our bathroom. In my pitiful state, I felt betrayed by God. I felt betrayed by myself. Had I been making up fairy tales in my mind? When I heard that voice say "it's over" after Josh's last brain surgery, was it just my imagination speaking to me, telling me what I wanted to believe? What if God wasn't with me? Obviously my mind was just playing tricks on me because nothing was over. *"Jesus I don't believe you anymore"*, my mouth muttered in a pool of tears.

At that moment, I felt the cold tile floor under my face turn to plush carpet and I was taken to a place far away from the *here and now.*

Startled, I stretched out my hand to push myself off the floor, but I couldn't. My fingers gripped strands of carpet as I tried to lift my head and scream out for help. But nothing would come out of my mouth - my voice no longer worked. That's when I knew it was over - 17 years old crawling across my mother's dining room floor. My body shut down and I could crawl no further. I desperately needed to reach her bedroom and wake her up. I wanted to live! I'd made a massive mistake, but the 38 pills that I'd swallowed earlier that night had already taken over my system, and there was no turning back now. I was done. It was over. I was going to die.

With my last thought, I prayed this prayer,

"God please forgive me for what I've done. Please God help me! In Jesus' name, Amen."


I'd never had an out of body experience before. I didn't believe in them quite honestly. My foolish cynical ways of the world were so strong, I'd even denied the night God had spared me from suicide. I never told anyone about what I'd experienced after my eyes were closed in finality on my mother's dining room floor. The memory I had of watching my step father shake me and try to wake me was vivid, yet far fetched from a testimony that anyone could believe. I'd seen my face, swollen and pale blue in color. I peered over Roger's shoulders watching my own lifeless body experiencing death.

From there I was taken to some sort of meeting room of sorts. It was a peaceful place - bright and full of light. There were others with me that knew me very well. They were sort of like a council of souls that were overseeing my life - they knew me even better than I knew myself.

"You have to go back. It's not your time yet. You have something important to do." This is the only message or conversation that I was able to obtain. Although I knew that I'd seen and heard many other things while I was in this state of consciousness - in a place far away from the world I'd left, when I fell asleep on my mother's dining room floor that night.

I never spoke about it to anyone. One of the paramedics on the scene at my mother's house came to visit me a few weeks after I returned home from the hospital - having no recollection of all of the procedures that were done in attempt to save my life. He said that he wanted to see me because he needed to see what a miracle looked like.

"Half of the drugs you ingested would have killed a 200 pound man. How are you here?" The older gentleman questioned me - his eyes were joyful and full of wonderment. I assumed he was looking for my testimony of the near death experience that I refused to give him. And following that visit, I started researching near death experiences.

So many stories I found - all kind of similar. People that had died say they saw a bright light (I guess I could call that place I saw "a bright light"). But unlike the others who say they saw Heaven with all of its beauty, I didn't remember seeing anything extraordinary. In fact, after reading through countless NDEs, I was convinced that I hadn't seen Heaven as they described - maybe I wasn't good enough to get in. I had witnessed a place that seemed more like a holding room or a panel of guides. And also different, I didn't have revelation like the others. I didn't wake up excited to tell others about God or about Jesus. I woke up angry that I was back in my miserable, purposeless 17 year old life. I didn't want to be here and I didn't feel any differently about God. As years went by, the whole thing seemed pointless. So what if I died and had an experience in the afterlife? It changed nothing in my life. *Not until now.*

As I awoke from the vision in a cloudy state of slumber, I heard, "How can you doubt me? I was the one who woke you." Peeling my face from the cold tile on our master bathroom floor, I felt confused and overwhelmed by what had just occurred. I had just been taken out of our bathroom and placed in a memory - literally I'd left my 36 year old body to revisit an experience from my past. It was so real, I could still smell the scent of my mother's home, as I settled back into my present surroundings. I leaned my back against wooden bathroom cabinets and digested the words I'd heard. I knew without a doubt who was speaking to me and I had finally received the answer that had lingered for nearly 20 years.

It never made sense really - how I even made it to my mother's dining room floor that night. After I had emptied two bottles of prescription pain pills down my throat, I'd fallen asleep at the kitchen table while writing a suicide note to my mom. Something woke me up. I know this because I was too far gone to be startled by anything. I couldn't see. I couldn't speak. Realizing how seriously hindered my brain was, I tried to get up and go get help. That's when I learned that my body didn't work anymore - I fell flat on my face, landing hard on the ground. My legs were like paper - they didn't respond. It took every bit of strength I could mustard up, to crawl a few feet to the dining room floor where I shut down completely.

238

What would have happened had I not woken up and prayed for forgiveness and help? *He woke me up.* He gave me that minute that I needed to realize that I had made a mistake - that I didn't want to die. He gave me a chance to cry out to God and ask for forgiveness. He gave me the opportunity to choose life. *Jesus was the one that woke me up.*

The reality of unexplainable happenings didn't matter anymore. Even today as I write this, completely aware that cynical minds, (people who think like me), will have a hard time believing in these supernatural experiences, it doesn't matter - they are more real to me than the air I breathe. And even more astonishing is the presence of God - so powerful and controlling, that in the bottom of my fear and pain and hopelessness; He immediately alters my mind, emotions and even circumstances.

In great peace and with an assurance of faith that was so strong, it couldn't have came from me, my doubt was suddenly and completely gone. Jesus - the one I can never doubt because He's the one who woke me up and saved my life all those years ago, said *"it's over."* And at that moment, my phone rang.

Dr. Dannenbaum's words echoed the spirt of God, on the other end of my cell phone. He said not to worry, the swelling and blood spots weren't worthy of a trip back to the medical center. "I'll tell you what. If you see anything of concern, I want you to text photos of Josh to my cell phone. If I feel like you need to bring him in, I'll let you know."

I climbed out of my blue jeans and threw on a pair of comfortable boxers, then turned off the lights throughout the house and closed the garage door.

I cleaned the blood from Josh's head and carefully switched out his pillow trying not to wake him. He looked up at me for a split second and then rolled over and continued in his snoring. "Goodnight sweetheart," I whispered, kissing Josh softly on the forehead.

That night I slept deeper and more peacefully than I had at any other time since we'd been home from the hospital. And the next morning, I received a text in response to the photos I'd sent to the doctor, reassuring me that Josh was healing just fine.

*And the peace of God, which passeth all understanding, shall keep your hearts and minds through Christ Jesus. - (Philippians 4:7)*

# Chapter Ten

# *Be* Still

## Healing in the Brokenness

When I was seventeen years old, God hit the *reset button* on my life. I never told anyone back then that I struggled with a strong sense of not belonging to this world. Even my mother had no idea at that time, that I would attempt suicide - and *almost* succeed.

That was also the year, when the Lord would later grant me the one thing that I'd asked him for since I was a 15-years old, drawing hearts in History class. He gave me Josh. Shortly after my near death experience, Josh and I started dating *seriously*, rented an apartment together and began a new chapter of life - in pursuit of *happily every after.*

Twenty years later, God hit the reset button on my life again. And even though this time, it was Josh that walked through that valley - I know it was my assignment to walk with him. It was my trial too.

In the journey at Josh's bedside, God was bringing me full circle back to the cross of Jesus, illuminating the very fear that had held me tightly in bondage for most of my adult life. He was teaching me that I control nothing, and showing me that trusting him wasn't just an option, it was *the only option.* He had taught me how to surrender to him. And somewhere deep inside of my thoughts, I expected this lesson to lead us to another *happily every after* - a miraculous healing over Josh.

In the weeks following Josh's final brain surgery, the dust from our tragedy began to settle - placing a heaviness upon our lives that was undeniably, heartbreaking.

I had hoped the final brain surgery would bring immediate change. But it didn't. Replacing Josh's skull chipped away nothing from the extensive list of physical deficits. He was still in a wheelchair, still unable to dress himself, feed himself or go to the bathroom on his own - among many other functions that were lost in the aftermath of severe brain damage. The wreckage of Josh's massive stroke, loomed over our lives daily. Our dreams for the future were gone - like broken glass, tossed away into the garbage. And my new role as a 24/7 caregiver was more difficult than I ever could've imagined.

On the outside, we had lost everything - our jobs, our hobbies, our friendships. Life didn't make sense anymore. And I battled through many days, wondering if the Lord had made a mistake.

*Surely, this isn't what you had planned for us God,* I would weep to myself, during the rare moments when I found time to be alone.

Picking up the pieces seemed impossible. And the heartfelt begging for God to let Josh live, soon transformed into a heartfelt begging to understand *why*.

I loaded Josh in the truck one Sunday morning and took him to our church. We hadn't been in public since the stroke. It was a new experience in many ways. I'd never witnessed so many people staring at us before. The attention didn't bother me really. I think what bothered me was that *why* that I struggled with, resounding in my thoughts as people glued their eyes to Josh and I. In my mind, I assumed that others were wondering what we must have done to receive such an awful sentence - how many sins we must have committed to land us in this cruel predicament.

When the worship band started the music, Josh began balling. I cried with him, not understanding the purpose of his tears. Crying was just something we did now, and we didn't have a need to discuss the reason.

242

The preacher that day talked about leading a happy marriage. His message was based upon scriptures in the new testament. Basically, he spoke about God's will for us to be happy - for our relationships to be beautiful and for our lives to reveal the goodness of his blessings.

I left church that day feeling rejected by God. Yet, something inside of me stirred viciously in confusion. I thought about all of the people we knew throughout our lives - people in our communities and even people in our church.

The time bomb ticking in my head continued as we settled in back at home. I thumbed through my Facebook wall, reading posts filled with family vacations and summer fun.

*Really God? That guy has probably never stepped foot in a church and he's got good health? Josh spent his spare time volunteering to coach kids. He deserves a stroke and this jerk is out on the boat today enjoying life?*

*What about her God? She's cheating on her husband with a guy at the gym, and look at the fun she's having laying on a tropical beach, while I'm here changing Josh's bedsheets.*

My thoughts were like a whirlwind of bitterness screaming out in anger at God. *It's not fair! We didn't deserve this!* - I told the Lord.

Later that evening, as I was cleaning up the mess from dinner, I received a text message from Bridget:

*On the way to the ER with Adam. He just had a massive seizure and he's not breathing. Please pray Jodi! Pray hard right now!*

I immediately dropped to my knees in our kitchen floor, grabbed Josh's right hand and began calling out to the Lord for mercy on Adam and Bridget. As my mind drifted into a place of meditation, words poured out of my lips in heartfelt desperation. And without me realizing what I was saying, my prayer ended in these words.

"Father, please let him live, in Jesus' name. Amen."

A sense of shock and deep sadness came over me, realizing what I had done. Like the Israelites, that followed Moses through the wilderness, murmuring and complaining along the way - I had forgotten the miracles he'd shown me. I let my focus drift from him parting the red sea and raining manna from the sky, to a place of bitterness and complaints.

As Josh and I sat on the patio together that evening, talking about Adam, a new kind of calmness came over me. I worried terribly about Bridget and hadn't heard anything from her since I'd received her frantic text message. But I knew the Lord was in control. And in that moment, I just wanted to be still - to enjoy the company of my sweet husband that the Lord had given to me *again*.

I wasn't thinking about the Facebook posts anymore - wondering why others were enjoying family vacations while we were stuck battling disability. I wasn't thinking about anything, except his mercy. It could've easily been us on our way to the ER that night, like Adam and Bridget. But it wasn't. God had let Josh live - and he was faithful when he told me "it's over." - never allowing us to step foot back into a dreadful emergency room after the final surgery.

We were home, safe and sound, enjoying beautiful music together, sitting poolside, hand in hand. Life had shown me that it can change in the blink of an eye. So tonight, I just want to sit still…..

**Blog Entry:** *The Blink of an Eye...*

It seems like we've spent our entire lives struggling to get to where we are going. There's always another goal, another milestone that we need to reach. Looking back, the memories flood through my mind in an instant - *a blink of an eye.* It's amazing how fast time has passed by. And as I search through our lives together thus far, the memories that I treasure the most are the ones where we had less.

Just a car full of clothes and a small U-haul truck with a few furniture pieces my mother donated, Josh and I got our first apartment together. That place was smaller than our master bedroom today - only about 500 square feet. We didn't know from day to day if we'd have enough money to pay the rent and utilities. I was working as a waitress and Josh had just started his manager in training position at Jiffy Lube. We survived off Ramen noodles and Dr. Pepper. Oh how I'd love to go back to that place - just to feel the carelessness that surrounds young love. Tomorrow just wasn't important to us back then. We lived in the moment, and loved every second of doing a whole of nothing - laughing at Jerry Springer episodes and battling against each other in front of a video console.

A year later, we had a mortgage and a baby on the way. Our wedding plans had to be moved up and our focus on the career-life became a fast reality. We needed more. We needed to *become* more. That's life's awful trick it plays - the misguided pursuit of things - cars, houses, stability.

Josh and I moved across six states in less than five years, chasing the American dream. He worked so hard and with every promotion we found a new home - each time diving into the unknown where we had no friends, no family, just us. That's all we needed.

I'm trying to figure out when everything changed - trying to remember when success became so important to us that I would develop a habit of staring at a computer screen until the early hours of morning - night after night. It's not that I don't think I'm a good wife or a good mother, although I could've done much better, I know. But I missed so much along the way. So many nights I forgot to see the stars, to hear the evening breeze and to feel the warmth of love that God had gifted to me. Some people spend their whole lives searching for what we've had all along - *love*. Life isn't about money or awards or promotions or even accomplishments. Life is about love. That's the greatest treasure of all.

I read a passage today from a traumatic brain injury survivor, posted on the blog on MariaKing.com. It said..

> *"It wasn't that long ago that I was running for my life. A distance of time and space. Or maybe running towards my new life. "Time waits for no man." The phrase is almost uncanny. Did you ever think that a life without regrets would be so scary? A life with no regrets is said too quickly."*

Those words were like the chapters of my life condensed into a place of utter sadness in realizing all that I'd taken for granted.

If I could go back 17 years and sit down with the teenager who knew everything, and couldn't wait for anything as she walked down the isle to marry the love of her life, I'd tell her, "Stay right here. Be still." I would hold his hand every chance I got. I'd spend less time working to become someone better than I was the day before, and I'd know that I already had everything I needed.

Tonight as I spend time with my love, who's trapped inside of a bad dream, I'll sit still. I'll savor these moments for the good and the bad and I'll take note of every breaking part of my heart that runs towards the new life that awaits us in a beautiful tomorrow.

I'll look to God and give thanks that I've been granted another chance to get it right. I'll see the stars and the moon and I'll feel the warmth of the summer breeze that dances across our patio, as we listen to music of our past. I'll embrace tomorrow and the promises of my savior, who knew that I'd be here long before I arrived.

May I never forget these moments - these nights when life stood still - the pain-stricken, knees to the floor, clinging to the rail of a hospital bed, with tears flowing so fast I could hardly breathe. And the hope I've found in a miracle created by God - a gift that no amount of success from a fallen world could ever compare to. May I never harbor regret for what I don't yet have, and may I cherish the beauty that surrounds me from this day, and forevermore.

The life behind me lives only in the blink of an eye. But the life before me will never slip away so briefly. Be still my heart. Be patient my soul. Part-two will be magnificent..... in the powerful name of Jesus.

---

In the valley, I learned that God is God. He's limitless, he's all-powerful and he's everywhere.

I learned that life can always be better than it is, and it can always be worse than it is. But regardless of where we are at in our journeys, he's in control.

I learned that brokenness can be meaningful - refining us and teaching us how to love others on a deeper level, with genuine compassion and purpose, beyond our understanding. I learned that pain can produce beauty - revealing all that we take for granted - teaching us how to suffer well, and rejoice in his goodness, even when we hurt.

I learned that life is full of detours and the unexpected can happen to anyone, at any time. But even in great loss and suffering, we can rest assure that God is using those detours, and planting purple stones in our paths along the way - leading us and guiding us to our final destination - our home in him.

I learned that life isn't all about *here and now,* but it's a masterful puzzle of his pieces, shifting all things into place for our eventual gain. And even in our worst moments, God is with us, teaching us, redeeming us and painting beauty with our ashes.

Most of all, I learned that Josh living wasn't the *big thing* I'd been searching for to perfect my faith. But the real miracle was in watching a masterful God peal away the layers of lies that I'd wrapped myself tightly into for most of my life. I learned that this broken world is full of broken systems - unreliable and imperfect. I learned that I control nothing, and fear is an illusion of ideas, lacking revelation from a sovereign God that never leaves my side.

Our three month journey through the valley, was only the beginning of God's plan to reveal truth in who we are and why we're here. In our tragedy, we were stripped away from our comfortable lives, in order for the Lord to draw us near to him and reveal himself in ways I'd never have believed were possible - had I not experienced him first-hand.

Like a journey through the wilderness, much like the Israelites, we walked through great uncertainty and fear, learning with every step, how to depend on God - and *only* on God. And while our storm is far from over, we're growing more each day in our faith - learning how to lay our troubles down at the cross - trusting in *His* will for our lives and understanding that there is freedom in surrendering to a God that loves us, cares for us, and heals our brokenness where it matters the most.. ....*our souls.*


*Though I walk in the midst of trouble, thou wilt revive me: thou shalt stretch forth thine hand against the wrath of mine enemies, and thy right hand shall save me. The Lord will perfect that which concerneth me: thy mercy, O Lord, endureth for ever: forsake not the works of thine own hands. - (Psalm 138:7-8)*

You can contact Jodi at <u>79ministry.com</u>

# *About* The Author

## Jodi Manfred

Jodi Manfred is a caregiver, wife, mother, real estate agent and public speaker, who first fell in love with the art of writing as a little girl. Writing poetry was her therapy - filling a void after her father left at her at the age of five.

Jodi reunited with her love for writing after her husband Josh suffered a massive stroke, and wasn't expected to live. At her husband's bedside, through two brain surgeries and several months in acute care hospitals, Jodi found a new first love - Jesus Christ.

Today, Jodi and her husband Josh work together through 79ministry.com, to give hope and encouragement to others who are suffering through difficult seasons of life. She also runs a blog, prayer services and bible studies. Jodi's real estate team in Houston, 79 Fine Homes, is named after her and her husband's temporary home, ICU ROOM #79, where her life was forever changed.

Her hope is to share the love of Jesus through her testimony and follow our Heavenly Father's will for her life, wherever he may lead.

**Note from Jodi:** *Thank you for reading our story. My prayer is that our continued testimony, as we learn each day how to carry our cross and follow Jesus, will touch your heart and encourage you. The Lord says the righteous will suffer many afflictions, but he promises to deliver us from them all, (Psalm 34:19). Stay strong in Jesus. He will finish our race!*

Made in the USA
Lexington, KY
10 April 2018